DIARY
of a Mad
Preschool
Teacher

Nonie Boyes

PAGE PUBLISHING, INC.
Conneaut Lake, PA

First originally published by Page Publishing 2021

ISBN 978-1-6624-1971-3 (pbk)
ISBN 978-1-6624-1972-0 (digital)

Printed in the United States of America

This story is dedicated to two heroes in my life who battled cancer on and off with strength, integrity, and courage. Thank you from the bottom of my heart and soul, Robert Bryant and Nick Vargas. They showed me the way.

Nonie Diary: 2011—2017

I have a tale to tell
Sometimes it gets so hard to hide it well
I was not ready for the fall
Too blind to see the writing on the wall
                    —Madonna, "Live to Tell"

Hello/Intro

THIS DIARY NOTES: 2011–2017 will help tell a tale I have wanted to tell for eight years. It's time for me to close this chapter of my life and hopefully help others who have dealt with witches and dragons and evil in a certain sense. Wrap it up, forgive, and try to forget. I learned a lot of life's lessons and hope you will too. Some of it are funny, some sad, and some unbelievable. But they did happen, and that is my story, and I'm sticking to them.

A big thank-you to my family who helped me through the three-plus years and to my preschool friends Barb, Elizabeth, and JL. I could not have done this without all your love and support.

Prologue

It All Started in Childhood

BEFORE I GIVE some insight on the three witches and my adventures, this is my turn to show myself as a youngster. It may explain a few things.

Humor, humor, humor. Even as a child, humor helped me through situations. That time I liked Tommy in fifth grade, but his friend did not like me for taking Tommy's attention away. I was so terribly thin and teased for years—wish that would be the case now. We would meet up at the park and swing on the swings. Both of us were very naive; that was about it, but we enjoyed talking and laughing—being silly, right up my alley.

One day, his friend Joey came too and was making fun of my legs, saying they looked like sticks. Tommy did not laugh and felt uncomfortable, so I told them I had polio when I was little and my one leg was thinner than the other. I walked ahead, and Joey said, "Oh, I am so sorry. I didn't know. I can see that your one leg is skinnier. Sorry." Well, that was not true at all, but I didn't want to hear it every time I saw him. I looked at it that I improvised. I tried to protect myself. Survival skills at the age of ten. I did go to confession and asked forgiveness on that one. Catholic guilt, another thing that nags at you no matter what age. Some wanted, some not.

In eighth grade in a very conservative Catholic school that I attended, there were a lot of discussions on which high school you would be attending. There were five children in my family, so high school was the public one nearby. Catholic school was expensive, and we all got that. This was looked down upon because everyone should continue their Catholic education, as the nuns would say. Many discussions went on, and I would be very quiet, uncomfortable, and afraid to tell anyone about the public school. The ones I did tell were friends of mine, and I would get an "Uh-oh," and the subject would go back to where *they* were going. That's okay, I was happy for them and did understand my mom and dad's decision. It was the other kids I had a problem with—the looks, whispers, and comments. So I decided to be ready in case I was asked again by casual people. My older sister and brother went to Lindblom Public High School, which was far from the house and not the public high school I would attend. I added a *saint* to it, and people would look puzzled and say, "I don't know that one."

I would say, "It's far. I would have to take two buses," which was the truth.

The questions stopped, and I let it go. Saint Lindblom. Nonie, honestly, was that necessary? At the time, yes. Another trip to the confessional.

With a little perseverance

You can get things done

Without the blind adherence

That has conquered some

And nobody wants to know you now

And nobody wants to show you how

So if you're lost and on your own

You can never surrender ("Never Surrender" by Corey Hart)

Chapter 1

The Story Unfolds

ONCE UPON A time in my younger days, I had not a care in the world when it came to teaching. I started out doing preschool classes when my children were young, and my organization was very flexible. My first boss was a wonderful woman named Cyndi who treated her employees with respect, and everyone loved her. She had such a nice demeanor but only stayed on for about five years.

As my children got older (school age), I was able to work more hours and loved every minute of it. The children and parents were great also, and every year, I learned more, took more early childhood classes to be more up-to-date, and met teachers who I am still friends with. Sounds too good to be true, but honestly, it was everything I could ask for and more.

That was when I met JL, and we did lesson plans together, did separate classes for eight years, then worked as a team for eight years. When employees walked by our room as we were getting ready for the day, they would say, "Too much levity in this room," and we all would laugh. But it was true; as a team, our chemistry made our classroom learning is fun.

Parents talk, which is good, and little by little, more calls came in asking to have their children be in our classes. What an achievement! Not only did we enjoy what we were doing but, most importantly, the kids loved us and we loved them. Everyone was a winner! We had families for years—starting with their eldest child to the youngest, getting to know them as our family. It was humbling.

We would talk and say how blessed we were. But reality was lurking around the corner in an unexpected place or places.

I have been told all my life by friends and family that I viewed life in rose-colored glasses. That is probably why I enjoyed preschool because being with the young, you do view life differently—more innocent, honest, but frank sometimes, like Mrs. Boyes. "How old are you? Why are you wearing that shirt? I don't like it. Do you and Mrs. J live here? Where are your beds? Where are your kids?"

Telling us stories of their lives at circle time. "Daddy slept on the couch, he had too many beers" My Mommy says bad words. I have 2 dogs (they had no pets, but the dogs had names), went to Disneyworld 3 times (never even left the state).

Even stories about how I threw up this morning, I have strep throat, my cat is in kitty heaven, he died. Which brings up lots and lots of conversation, trying to move on, when no one cares what day it is or month, priceless moments, but we would be masters on how to reroute the conversation. We had to look away or try not to laugh at some of the things mentioned. It was magical!

No matter what age I am, there still is that "little mischievous gleam in my eye," to have humor in all situations which gets me to this point and beyond. Would never had made it without humor, family and friends, and prayers, never!

Because I'm happy

Clap along if you feel like happiness is the truth
("Happy" by Pharrell Williams)

Chapter 2

The Early Days/The Good Bosses

WE MOVED TO our new house in a wonderful town with great schools, lots of young families with kids, good parks, near highways, and a train station for my husband's job. I was very fortunate to be able to stay at home with my two children until my daughter was in school. Life was good—our parents were alive, our families were tight, there were some money issues, but with some finagling, we managed.

I met some people in our area through church, and one in particular, Debbie, was babysitting in another church and said they were looking for help. My son was in school, and my daughter was two, but I could bring her with me. Two days a week, three hours a day kept me busy. My daughter had kids to play with, and I made a little money. Good mixture. Debbie got a job at the preschool, and when my daughter turned three, she said they needed help. I went for an interview with Cyndi, who I mentioned earlier. She was a super nice person, easy to talk to. I got the job. While my daughter was in a different preschool, which was super close to our home and where neighborhood children went to, I started working early childhood classes. The preschool was in a building stage, and I actually incorporated a few classes which lasted ten-plus years to their program. I only worked two days a week, three hours a day at first when my daughter was in school. The next year, I worked three days a week for three hours a day. I absolutely loved it. I had done subbing here and there in our old house and really missed being with the children, having a room to decorate, and being creative.

Once my daughter went to kindergarten, I started working every day but only in the morning. It was a perfect job; Cyndi was flexible. I got the best of both worlds, home and work.

Once my daughter was in school full time, I started working two afternoons a week so I could help out at my son's class and hers on my afternoons off. Again, it was great, and I met many wonderful families and children with classes in ages two through five. I was able to implement more early childhood classes (I developed some that lasted ten years or so) with science, math, storytelling, etc. I never got bored; doing them actually taught me a lot. People think, *It's just preschool classes*, but a lot of research goes into them—reviewing dinosaurs, travels to different countries, science experiments (that was hardest for me; not very scientific in my brain, but I learned). Music and storytelling were my favorites and arts and crafts with every imaginable piece of material you could find. All that work was therapeutic for me. Cyndi loved that my budgets were always on the low side, and she loved the creativity. Loved doing lesson plans, and eventually, I was put in charge of some of the other teachers to run the meetings. I did not get any extra money for that, but the challenge was strongly embraced. You really do learn a lot when you get people together, and picking at one another's brains was intoxicating. Plus we formed friendships from those get-togethers.

Cyndi found a better job for herself and left the preschool the next fall. I worked under her for four-plus years and was very lucky to have such a nice, respectful boss. She warned me about some of the other bosses there and said, "Watch your back." I know women can be catty at times, but if you haven't walked in someone else's shoes, you don't really know. You learn though—some quicker than others. I was a little slow. Sloth slow. Yeah, that bad.

Andy was my next boss and wanted me to broaden my classes and asked if I would be willing to do an exercise class and gym class. I was never very good in gym class but was told I would be working with a retired gym teacher. Donna was very good, a little strict, but the children listened to her. There were three classes back to back, and boy, did I get a workout. The children's ages were four to six. They were so sweet and wanting to please. It was a great experience. I learned a lot—spotting, foot positioning, and was even able to stand on my head. I hadn't done that since high school. I worked hard, and it was definitely beneficial to the children and myself. I had fun. "Mrs. Boyes, look at me. No, look at me." I almost got whiplash turning my head from one to another. We had an end-of-the-year show where parents got to watch what they learned. They were very appreciative, and Donna and I got great ratings. Never thought I could do it, but I did and am glad I did. In life, you have to try new things, and with each learning experience, you can be better than before.

After three years with Andy now as our boss, many early childhood teachers came and went, but then I met JL. I did not realize her daughter was in one of the gym classes—a real sweetie, Hallie, who really liked me. JL was put in to work on early childhood classes, and we clicked on day 1. She did some of the same classes as I did in a different facility, some twos with parents and three- and four-year-olds without parents. Her humor was a bit like mine, sometimes dry and sometimes just out-there. We did lesson plans together along with three other teachers, and everyone added something new and special to the mix. Andy was pleased. We kept the budget low, added things from home (all teachers do that), and used whatever we could find in the art-craft closet. Things worked for years, but now my children are older, and so are JL's. We were looking into the preschool.

The preschool had a teacher-in-charge for many years. Abby was always nice at meetings, but rumor had it that it was her way or no way. JL really wanted to try it. We would be able to be team teaching, and we both knew that would not be a problem, so we talked to Andy about our interest. She was skeptical about it because she said "It's a whole different animal" there from what we were used to. She also needed early childhood teachers and liked the fact there were waiting lists for many of both our classes. We suggested that we would still do early childhood classes in the morning, but if an afternoon preschool class opened, we would like to teach that. So in the late summer of that year, two teachers left, and we got the job! More regular hours plus more hours for planning time. Sounds like a match made in heaven, right? Well, it took a little time to adjust not to the class but to all the rules that Abby had. She did a fantastic job though, super organized. The preschool was a ship, and she was the captain. As long as you did what you were told, everyone was happy. We were new at this, so we did exactly that. It did work, except there was some unrest among some of the teachers. Jealousy too. You needed to watch your words, and if you were told something unpleasant, just forget it. This went on for two years, but we learned a lot about people and all those behind-the-scene moments.

Then Andy got a promotion, and we got a new boss, Micki. She was way too nice and wanted to change up the preschool. There were a lot of pull-and-tug moments, some crying moments, especially with poor Micki. JL and I were torn. We got to like Abby; maybe her tactics were a bit strong at times, but the preschool did work well and parents gave rave reviews year after year. The problem was, Abby thought she was a boss, and she was not. No one ever stepped in her way until Micki, and Micki just had a different approach, a less-structured approach. Both were right, but someone had to give. Micki was the boss, and change was not a bad thing, but not in Abby's eyes. Abby had quite a few preschool teachers who were her friends and would die for her. The only bad thing is, they did it the wrong way. They told parents about it. Preschool 101. Never, never talk to parents about management. They wanted the parents to complain about the changes being made, and they did just that. JL and I were at a different facility, and we were glad. We did like some of the changes Micki was going to incorporate in the classroom—more stations, dramatic play, less structure. We even started doing them. Every time you get a new boss, things change. This did not go well with Abby. More teachers talking mutiny. It was an awkward time for JL and me. We liked Abby, but we truly liked Micki and her ideas. We told Abby we would do whatever was to come. We were only at the preschool for two years and really loved it. We did not want to rock the boat. We would sail wherever they wanted.

In the meantime, our friend Barb became Micki's assistant. She was between a rock and a hard place, too, because she knew everyone well enough but felt Micki was in the right and that the preschool needed to expand its way of teaching. Micki's boss got a hold of all that was going on (it wasn't pretty), and Abby was talked to. Micki, in turn, only lasted the year. She was so upset all this was going on, all the calls and the dissension among half of the teachers. Just terrible. Barb said she cried on and off that whole year.

She did not deserve that, not in that way. It should have been handled differently by communication. We felt horrible for her. She knew we were in a tight situation, too, but we told her we would do whatever was best for the preschool. She appreciated our input but left before the next school year started. Two other teachers left (friends of Abby) that summer, and Abby resigned also. A change was a coming.

One good thing out of all this mess was, we got more preschool hours and were working mornings, five days a week and afternoons, three days a week. Not how we wanted to get those hours, but it is what it is. We were happy for ourselves but not happy on the whole situation.

At that time, we got Marie as our boss until they hired a permanent preschool manager. She worked at the preschool in the maintenance division and worked with camps all year round for grade-school children. She was feisty, in a good way, and had a funny humor about her, but I would not want to cross her. JL and I got along with her nicely, no problems, but in meetings, she was very blunt as to what she wanted. The teachers complied. Marie did not change things up very much because she knew she would not be our boss for long. She did fight for us when it came to salary and gave everyone a large raise. She had done research in the surrounding suburbs and found we were being paid less than most. All the teachers rallied around her after that. She was a fair boss. Never in all the years of working there did that happen again. At the end of the year every year, we would get small raises on merit. Every now and then, the preschool teachers would get one for cost of living. She only was our boss for nine months. Marie and her family moved out of state because of her husband's job. We all respected her and missed her, too. I think of her time and again and hope all is well with her and her family.

A new boss was hired after Marie left: Shelley, who was nice but a little different. You just couldn't figure her out; she was more serious, not much of a sense of humor, and with all the changes, everyone was treading lightly. Thank goodness Barb was still our assistant manager, never wanting the main job but she would give us insight on Shelley, and we grew to like her. Some people are just hard to read, and first impressions can be wrong. She made changes adding to Micki's changes—room setups, less-structured art projects (yay), parent-teacher conferences, different ways to do bulletin boards, staff taking extracurricular classes (great idea), and more. Some of the teachers did not like the changes and left after a year. JL and I liked the changes and brought more creative juices to the table.

My father had died suddenly that year, and Shelley was absolutely wonderful to me. She gave me time off and even asked how I was doing on and off. She confided in me about how she had lost her mom a few years ago (which we did not know) and was very comforting. I sincerely appreciated that. She only stayed for two-plus years and moved on. Barb was our boss for the remaining year. What was next?

The preschool hired a perky, wonderful preschool manager named Carol. Carol was young, full of ideas, and very enthusiastic. She even took us out for a dinner (on her) to get to know each one of us in a casual setting. We never had that before. EVERYONE loved her. She took notes on any ideas any of us had, what worked and what didn't. She was amazing and very easy to talk to. She really liked the idea of the teachers taking extra classes and going to seminars. We needed a certain number per year, and no one complained. All that extra learning was very beneficial in the classroom. Barb liked working with her too. Everything was running smoothly. Lots of respect both ways. This lasted two-plus years because Carol became pregnant with twins. They ran in her family, but she told us she still planned on working after the babies were born. Some complications occurred, however, and she needed bedrest for her last month. Barb took over; she knew the job well enough, so no problems. Smooth sailing. After the beginning of the year when her maternity leave was up, she chose not to come back. We never got to talk with her. I don't think there were any medical reasons, probably just needed to stay home with her new babies. Upper management did not talk to us about it, and Barb knew nothing either. We never got to say goodbye and good luck. Sad and a bit mysterious, but privacy act does protect the employee. We just liked her so much, and even though she wasn't our boss for long, she was greatly missed. All best wishes to her and her family. Some teachers still talked about her for years. That was a great boss.

For the next school year in August, the preschool hired Janice as our preschool manager. She lived near me, but I did not know her though. She was pleasant, but no Carol. Barb was growing tired of bosses in and out, and she decided to leave. She was greatly missed. She would get all our supplies, was always on time, and was very respectful to all teachers and parents and children. What wasn't to like? She was also a good friend to JL and me and was never, never partial to us. Everyone was treated alike, like it should be in any place of employment. She would come into the classes twice a year and evaluate us, our room, etc. She would never let you know when she was coming. This was a good thing because as teachers, you sometimes could use constructive criticism to help your teaching skills, decorating skills, etc. Barb was courteous to the point of being kind in her delivery on improvements. I don't think anyone disapproved of the way she did her job. She was the backbone of the preschool for many years and would be missed by all.

Janice had a meeker demeanor, quiet but nice. She did have younger children at home, so she never could stay after school if there was a problem you wanted to discuss. She believed in email and relied on it for most of the communication among teachers. She had to do the buying of supplies, too, and we would not get our supplies on time. We had to go and pick them up at her office; she would not deliver them to our rooms. We were spoiled by Barb all those years, but we all adjusted.

The meetings were shorter, once a month, and some things got pushed to the side, and then miscommunication set in. Janice stayed only two years. I am sure it was taxing on her because the hours were more than she wanted. Saw her now and then at the grocery store. She ended up getting a job in the library at a grade school and loved it.

It was just that as soon as we got used to a manager, they were gone for one reason or another. Also, each manager wanted it the way they saw it (understandable), but it was a little difficult for the teachers. As soon as you adjusted to one, poof, they were gone. Teachers were leaving for all different reasons, and the turnover was big. The whole preschool was changing in every way possible. Half of the staff was now new teachers—not a bad thing, just different than what JL and I were used to. We were the older lot now. A lot of the families were the same, and enrollment was still good. That was important. We had steady jobs that we loved and had each other as team teachers. Learned to be more flexible, which is a good thing in life. That life lesson helped me as the years continued.

Another person from the preschool who also did camps for children ten-plus and after-school programs became our boss. Joanie was nice enough; we knew her for many years, but not well. Joanie had a medical condition years back, and I did send her a card with best wishes at that time. She really did not want the job, so I heard, but did a good job for the short time she was there, approximately nine months. She had a heavy schedule still doing her other jobs but kept the preschool moving along. We were on our own a lot; she overlooked our meetings and was there if there was a problem. Nothing bad happened on her watch. The preschool teachers plugged along pretty well. It was a good year, so nothing major. Quiet, I like quiet.

People

People who need people

*Are the luckiest people in the world ("People,"
Barbra Streisand)*

Chapter 3

The First and Second Witch Appear

Witch Number 1: Sunny

WE ALL WERE wondering if we were ever going to get a boss who would stay five-plus years. Change after change in such little timeframe was grueling at times. Well, we got what we wished for. Here came Sunny who lasted five years. She broke the record and broke my heart. It got a little darker each year, and the preschool was surrounded with a forest that went wild. "Watch what you wish for"—isn't that a saying that says it all? Yes, indeed, at least for me.

When Sunny was hired four years prior, she was sweet and bubbly and super friendly. Almost to a fault. I learned about her boyfriend who married her girl friend and how she was crushed—too much info—and how he was not happy and wanted to be with her blah, blah, kind of like *The Bachelor* with lots of drama. I would listen, and she then showed darker sides of herself (which we all have) about how she wanted him back and he wanted her and that she would do anything for that to happen. "ANYTHING," she kept saying. They did get back together; don't know the details, and don't want to.

I gave very little advice. She was my boss; it was awkward. She was close to my son's age. I just listened but got the feeling that she had some self-doubt issues, self-esteem, too, which started when she was young. She was always wanting to please her dad but never feeling she got enough attention and even said she could be a mean girl if need be and questioned about the way she looked etc. She was cute with a nice smile, but she warned me one day that she was good at hiding her true feelings and that if anyone ever tried to cross her or if she felt they were not on her side, she would show no mercy! Great, why did I not remember that when she was firing teachers and got after me. Too late. She did end up with her boyfriend, who became her husband, and never spoke to the girl friend again. I felt bad for everyone in that relationship.

I have my own issues, not a psychologist by any means, but I do believe when someone tries to make you look bad or beneath them in some way, it makes them feel better about themselves. A bit warped way of thinking, but, psychology 101, it's in there as true. I hope she found happiness and will remember my mom's words, "If you can't say anything nice, don't say it at all," for her sake and her children. That was what made it a little easier for me to understand my situation at hand. The potion was being made.

This happened right before Sunny left on maternity leave.

The new ruling was that each teacher gets together with another teacher from a different building to make lesson plans for one month. We were given the theme but had to incorporate the threes and fours on a weekly theme with a given letter of the week, such as letter G for March, do green projects. It sounds complicated, but in reality, it was fun, and we got a lot of creative juices flowing.

I was teamed with Stacey, a newer teacher who I worked with once when she subbed for JL. She was young, nice, and full of ideas! We talked on the phone twice and got together twice to put month together. She did the threes, and I did the fours only because she had two three-year-old-classes to my one, and I had two four-year-old classes with her one.

She really wanted to do houses, which I did not because the letter H was not done yet but would be in the next coming months. So she did houses that were red for the letter R, and I did roads that were red. We laughed and said it was like doing a colorful neighborhood.

We copied our plans to Sunny because they needed approval. We did not hear anything, which many times happened, till one week before the month.

JL came in the room before class and was acting off. I asked her if everything was okay, and she said yes. Didn't think much of it; with the children in the room, there was no time to ponder, but then came lunchtime. We had forty minutes till our next class, and she said she needed to tell me something. I got worried because I knew her family and was hoping everyone was okay. She said, "I want to show you something," and pulled out what looked like an email. "Read this," she said. "I wasn't going to say anything, but it really bothers me, and I feel you should know."

"Okay," I said nervously and read it. It wasn't long, but I had to read it three times to believe it. My boss, Sunny, sent an email asking JL and two other teachers if they knew if I and Stacey had gotten together for lesson plans because we were not in sync with each other. What? Stacey and I had not gotten any info from her, and she was asking the teacher I worked with if I planned with another teacher? Insane! Just ask us if there was a problem. That was overstepping the bound of professionalism. Is there such a thing as mole-ism, like checking up on other people behind your back? Obviously.

JL showed me the email she sent back to Sunny saying, "I know for a fact they got together twice at our room and talked on the phone. Please refer to Mrs. Boyes, thank you."

Nothing back. I then said, "I am going to let Stacey know, and we will talk to Sunny to straighten out whatever needs to be straightened."

I called Stacey after school and asked if she could meet me the next day.

"Is there a problem?"

"Sort of," I said, "but nothing big."

She came, and I showed her the email after JL went home. She was angry! "What are we going to do?" I said.

"We need to talk to Sunny."

So we did. We called and asked if we could stop by her office. Stacey started with "How can you send an email about our work to someone else?" Sunny played dumb until I told her I found the email in JL's lesson plans while looking for ours. I did not want JL to be in any kind of trouble. Sunny stuttered and hemmed and hawed and said she did not think we got together for all the plans. Stacey mentioned how she really wanted to do houses, and Mrs. Boyes wanted to do roads and felt it was like a neighborhood thing. Sunny did not look at us both, looked down, but did not apologize for sending and checking up on us through JL's email. "Why didn't you come to us?" asked Stacey, who was visibly angry. "Why would you tell other teachers what you felt and not us?"

"I was going to," she said, and nothing else.

I said, "Do you want us to redo part of the lesson plans?"

"No, I get where you were coming from now." She put her coat on and said she had to go.

We sat there for a few minutes and looked at each other. Stacey said, "I don't like this at all. She did not even apologize."

I said, "I know, but she probably will not do that again."

Stacey said, "She won't with me. I cannot work with someone I do not trust." After our month of plans were implemented, Stacey gave her two-week notice. Sunny sent an email to all teachers that her computer blew up, and she lost all emails. Interesting. Convenient. I kept some of mine just in case I would need them. Many had a ton, or plenty, of discrepancies from one week to the next, really? Sunny went on her maternity leave, and Anna was in charge. It was going from bad witch to worse witch. "Auntie Em, it's a twister, it's a twister."

Time is supposed to heal

Ain't done much healing ("Hello" by Adele)

Witch Number 2: Anna

We had lesson plans that needed to be turned in by the twenty-first of the month. Anna called during JL and my class and said she needed the plans today. "Do you have them ready?" I replied yes, that I would bring them after class that day, which was 3:30 p.m. She said she needed them immediately and would come and pick them up. She never came, so at 3:30 p.m., I dropped them off. She laughed saying, "Oh, I thought it was the twenty-first, not the twentieth." JL and I were worried all day, thinking, *Now what?* Anna had a way to make you feel like you did something wrong when it was nothing.

Another example: Sunny and Anna made up a list of themes per month and who would be working on them. They liked to pair up teachers from different facilities, no problem. The plans needed to be done by the fifteenth or so, and it was the twelfth of November. JL had already done the planning, and Anna called her and asked if she could do January instead of December's plans. Nicely, JL told her that she had done the plans already. Anna went on and said how easy a month December was because there were only three weeks instead of four. JL just listened and again said the plans were already done. At a meeting in December, Anna went on and on about what a great teacher El was because she took on January plus her desig-nated month of March. She kept going on and how we needed to be more flexible and more like El, looking at JL. JL was mad about that because she was always helping out, too, but Anna was just making a point. El, on the other hand, had no idea what was going on and did not do that for any recognition. Anna just had a way to stir that pot of no-good potion. It did not work, however, because both JL and I stayed friends with El all the years we were there.

Anna came into our room as we were decorating, and one of the other teachers, Joan, showed her how we put up new backing to hold the art projects better. Anna said that Sunny said to take it down. Funny, because we all asked Sunny about it first, and she said it would be fine. Anna said she would get back to us and "be pre-pared to change it." Two days later, Sunny came in alone and loved it. Nothing else was said about it from Anna. Drama, drama, drama, just to make us question ourselves time and time again.

Placed order for supplies on the twentieth of the month. We had asked for paints and were told they were on back order by Anna. The same afternoon, Anna brought in the paints and said she gave us extra because there was an overabundance of paint all of a sudden. JL went through the box after class, and it was just our order, no extras. Never knew what to believe or not. What a rigamarole!

March's theme usually had to do with health. We were told by Anna that March would be called Healthy Me, dealing with body, nutrition, and teeth. Sounded good. Mary and El called us and said that Anna said we said it was too much for one month and should be divided into two months. We just heard from Anna about the theme probably an hour ago. What changed? We told them we never said that and would do whatever Sunny and Anna wanted. It took three phone calls to straighten out the "miscommunication," and when we saw Anna, she played dumb and said to do it in the one-month time period. What was all that about? Unnecessary craziness. Complete chaos.

Anna came to one of the camps and dropped off our food supply. While I was putting things in the closet, Anna asked JL if she had Joan's phone number. Anna was having a problem with Joan at the time. Joan was very assertive and would call her out with mixed messages to the teachers and other issues. She was a very good teacher and a fun person. She had no idea who she was dealing with at the time; no one did. JL and I knew of all this, so JL said she did not have her number. But wasn't there a phone list of all the teachers? Anna said that Sunny had deleted them by accident. That sounded a bit suspicious, but JL held her ground and told her, "Sorry." She did not want to help her in a witch hunt. JL went to drop off something at Sunny's office, and there on the bulletin board was a sheet with all the teacher's numbers. Some teachers at the time only wanted their landline available, not their cell number. Joan was one of them who chose to do that. Anna wanted her cell number but would have to get it from someone else. Never knew what that was all about, but Joan lasted a year and a half and left. JL and I missed her. Don't think management did.

Anna came in many times during our class time. I did not like it; she wanted to talk, but it was not the time to do that, in my opinion. Again, JL would talk to her, and I would be with the children. She could pull it off, her being more polite than me. I strongly felt class time was our time with the children, and unless it was an emergency, we could wait and talk at lunch or before or after class. It was close to the end of class one time, and Anna waited around as if she had something on her mind. When everyone left, she said, "Don't complain when I come into your room unannounced."

"Where did you get that information?" I asked.

She stuttered a little, and you could see she was uncomfortable. About a month earlier, JL and I had lunch one day with Mary and El. That topic was discussed, and everyone felt the same way. At least we thought. Someone said something, and here we are. "Well, it just seems that you do not want to talk when I come in."

I looked at JL and said, "I just don't like to take time away from our class and children. Even JL and I wait to talk about things after class."

"Oh, I see," she said.

Nothing changed though; she still came in and disrupted our class like a whirlwind. I just chose not to be a part of it. That decision probably hurt me. Remember the saying "Keep your friends close and your enemies closer." I sincerely did not feel she was my enemy at the time, but she was not a friend either.

It was near Mother's Day, and Anna came in with our last book orders. The subject came up about a Mother's Day tea, and JL told her we were not going to do one because the other facility decided not to do one either. This was a time when Anna was our boss during Sunny's maternity leave, so there was a lot of confusion about doing a tea or not. We were not given any true direction. The other facility said no, so we said, to be on the same page, we would not do it either. At the other facility were Katrina and Margie, both only working at the preschool for two years. Katrina was the teacher who worked with me a year later and was the mole.

Anna then said, "Yes, they are doing one. You better get the right information." After class, JL called Katrina and Margie and asked them again about the tea. They said they were having the moms come in the last ten minutes of class so the children could sing a few songs and give them a flower all the teachers had planted with the kids.

"Okay, great," said JL, "we will do the same."

Katrina replied, "Gee, that's funny because Anna told us that you two were doing the tea."

JL was furious but contained herself. "No, we will do what was planned and be on the same page."

Katrina was happy to hear that, and after that day, it was never mentioned again. Ahh!

> *I find it hard to tell you*
>
> *Cause I find it hard to take*
>
> *When people run in circles, it's a very, very*
>
> *Mad World*
>
> *Mad World ("Mad World" by Gary Jules)*

Chapter 4

Behind the Preschool Scenes

THIS WAS WHERE the madness began.

Once upon a time, there were three witches who had power over the preschool. They did not look like witches, were pretty to look at, and said all the right things when it was necessary. To your face, they seemed like they cared, and maybe they did sometimes, but when push came to shove, they installed moles in rooms to tattle and watch over certain teachers. One of them was me. There were others who quit or were fired on hearsay, but you never thought it was going to happen to you.

So it all started when I had an old neighbor, Anna, who moved back to our town. Heard stories about her—how she talked about people in the neighborhood at bridge games, etc., and was merciless. My daughter babysat her son once or twice and felt uncomfortable there. All she said was, something wasn't right. I never had her go back, but she would decline nicely when asked.

Saw Anna in a store parking lot after seven years or so. Her family just moved back to the area and told her there was a job opening at the preschool as assistant manager, figuring after seven years, everyone should get a second chance, and nothing happened to me personally. So she went and got the job. Little did I know that there was a witch who had magical, hypnotizing powers in our midst. The web was beginning to form before I knew it.

As JL and I were getting our room ready for class to begin in three weeks, Anna came in, told her congrats, and started to talk about viewing another preschool and how they had chairs on wheels for the teachers to get from one side of the table to the next. I then proceeded to say how that saves your back, instead of us sitting on the small chairs. She smiled and agreed, and both JL and I were going to bring it up at our next meeting as a suggestion.

Well, the next day, I got an email from my boss to come to her office. I always have had a good relationship with her, so I did not think too much of it. When I arrived, my boss, her boss (who I knew well), and human resource were there. My first words were "What's going on?" I was questioned for about ten minutes. How was my back? Do I have back issues? Have I ever needed a brace? I do have minor lower back issues, pull glutes, etc., but then the chair was brought up. "Can you only work with that type of chair?"

I said, "No, but we saw them at another preschool [which was a field trip from our organization] and thought they were a good idea."

My boss's boss, Brainard, seemed annoyed he was called in. I said I just mentioned it in passing. My boss said it would not happen due to funds. I said, "Okay. Again, I just mentioned it in a casual conversation. Another preschool had them. The teachers loved them, so I thought it was worth bringing up." WRONG! Did not realize this could cause such commotion. That was a lesson I should have learned but didn't. Anna was good at stirring the pot, and the potion was deadly. This was the lull before the storm. Little did I know a tsunami was coming.

Somethings happening here

What it is ain't exactly clear ("For What It's Worth" Buffalo Springfield)

Chapter 5

Stuck in the Middle with You

EVERYTHING STARTED TO change that year. Supplies were lost, and both JL and I were at fault. Anna was in charge of supplies and our rooms. She would say she left them on our counters, which they were not, only to find them in her car two days later. No apologies. She would come in and look at bulletin boards and tell us to do one thing and then come back when they were completed and tell us to change them. One time, she came in fifteen minutes before class, said Sunny did not want ABCs on bulletin board, took one side of it with children's artwork on it, and tore it off the wall! Our class started in fifteen minutes! We were running around cleaning up like chickens with our heads cut off. Our children's artworks were on those bulletin boards! I was trembling with fear and anger. What's next? If you think you have seen it all, you haven't. Both JL and I were terrified. You did not know what to expect from day to day. Yet at meetings, everything seemed okay for a while. In front of a group, she seemed in control, nice, but brought a lot of mixed feelings from one month to the next. As soon as you had your guard down, rumors were flying that teachers were going to be fired. Just as women do, we would all talk, but some teachers were very friendly with Anna. So as my mom used to say, "If you can't say anything nice, don't say anything." But being human, a few things were said all around, me included, and now meetings were starting to get hostile.

One time, we were at a meeting at a local library, and Sunny, my boss, started out the meeting with, "I know some people are not happy here, so if you don't like what is going on, leave!" She said she would find out who was being insubordinate if that was the last thing she did. Wow! Insubordinate? Who? Teachers were just plain scared, not knowing what would happen next. Now everyone was on the list. By the end of the year, two people were fired and one left. In the twenty years or so I had worked prior, one teacher was fired and a few left because of retirement, better money and benefits, or moving. Crazy times! You were always watching your back. Thank God I had JL, but our next year together was the last.

My boss, Sunny, went on maternity leave, which made Anna the one in charge of everything. She would come in and talk about the other teachers, pure gossip. Even teachers she was very friendly with, she would go on and on about how they didn't do this right, etc. A boss does not do that. You know that if she was telling us things about others, she was talking about us also. This made it a very uncomfortable setting. I started really distancing myself from her conversations because of the negativity, but she took my actions as unfriendly—that's what other teachers told me. And that's when things spiraled. Didn't know what was up or down anymore, what was right or wrong.

I told JL and other teachers, when asked why I wasn't talking to Anna, that I felt safer not to and did not want anything misconstrued. Well, that sure backfired when another preschool teacher or two told Anna that Mrs. Boyes was keeping distance because she did not want any problems. Speaking the truth is not always the right thing to do. I was doomed.

An example was the day we had parent-teacher conferences and got a phone call from Anna. JL answered the phone. Anna asked for me, and when I got on the phone, she started screaming at me about lesson plans with another teacher, named Lee. I tried to talk, but she was yelling so loud. JL took the phone and, literally after a minute, told her, "This is JL. Mrs. Boyes is crying. You need to calm down right now." Anna really knew how to stir the pot. Whatever she was cooking, you didn't want to try it. She was in a tizzy.

Anna asked to talk to me again. I went back to the phone, and she was calm as can be, saying, "I know you did the lesson plans, but I don't think Lee, did. And you are a great teacher blah, blah, blah…" Yikes! Who was that on the phone—one minute a witch worse than Sleeping Beauty's Maleficent and then a person complimenting me? What a shuckle, muckle mess! She only did that because JL was there and could hear and view everything that was happening. She was trying to cover her tracks. It must have been exhausting.

If it were not for JL, I would not have gotten through the parent-teacher conferences that day. God was with me too. The ironic thing is that the other teacher did lesson plans with me, and we talked twice and got together once to coordinate them. Why didn't she call her up?

One other time prior to that incident, Anna was in our room telling us how to do something in our plans, and I spoke explaining what we were doing, but she continued walking with her back to me (as if she did not care to hear what I had to say) and gave me a backhand wave, dismissing my opinion and basically making me feel like "I don't want to hear it. Your words are nothing." I did send an email to my boss, Sunny, who was on maternity leave, telling her what happened but never heard from her. At least not then. Lots of spooky things lurking in the deep, dark forest that was swallowing up the preschool, but could no one else see it but me?

Time changes everything

One truth always stays the same

You're still you after, all you're still you ("You're Still You" Josh Groban)

Chapter 6

Help, I Need Somebody, Anybody

IT WAS JANUARY, and all the stress was getting to JL and I. She got a bad cold but was feeling better.

I started feeling ill—I mean, not just mentally and emotionally but physically drained. Having sinus issues, I thought it was just my sinuses, but sure enough, I started to get a cough. I let it go like we all do and plugged away, but when I started to run a fever, I went to the doctor. I had walking pneumonia! It was a Friday, and our preschool was in a district that had a Teacher's Institute Day, so no school. Talked to JL, and she said, "You have to tell Anna. She will get you subs." So I called her and gave her a message about me having walking pneumonia and would not be coming in next week. Saturday rolled around, no call back; emailed her, no response. It was Sunday morning, and I couldn't even get out of bed, so my husband sent one more email. By afternoon, I hardly had any voice from the coughing but called two teachers who would sub for me.

On Monday morning, we had six inches of snow and falling, so school was shut down. I got an email from Anna stating, "You need a doctor's note if you are going to be off all week." That was the only communication I got. It snowed Tuesday night, and school was called off for Wednesday too. No calls to see how I was. One of the preschool teachers, Mary, told me in an email that Anna was supposed to get us subs when we are ill. I had not taken a day off in a few years, so I did not know that. It was offered nonchalantly when I got back to class. "Oh, you should have let me get you subs," said Anna in a meeting where everyone was present. I did not reply. How could I?

When I came back the next week, I did not look too good. My coloring was pale to say the least. When I came home, I would take a nap for an hour plus. If things were better at the preschool, I would have taken two extra days, but I knew anything and everything could be taken against me. Parents were asking, "Are you okay?" I had a very pale color for at least a month. I said the doctor said it would take time, but the cough was almost gone. Three weeks later, I saw my bosses' boss, Frank, and he asked how I was feeling. He even mentioned to JL that I did not look so good. Anna never came in our room or contacted me until the monthly meeting and, in front of everyone, asked how I was. Perception is a funny thing. You have to laugh.

There was still this chill in the air as summer was upon us. JL and I did summer camps together for the last few years, and we asked to do them again. We received a not-so-funny email stating the summer camp was going to be more strenuous this year, so Sunny decided to go with college students. Said she was looking out for our health. Okay, sure. I will go deeper into this later.

I wish for just one day that you could stand inside my shoes

And just for that moment I could be you

Yes, I wish for just that one time you could stand inside my shoes

You'd know what a drag it is to see you ("Positively 4th Street" by Bob Dylan)

Chapter 7

Meeting with Sunny, Brainard, and Me

SUMMER WAS GOOD, except I got a letter from Sunny that I needed to come in to talk. So I came in, and there was Sunny and her boss. Now what? Anna wrote up six problem areas I was having and things I said. Where's Anna? She always lurked in the shadows, but I didn't see her (I thought this but did not say it). Did ask why she was not there. "She is afraid of you," said Sunny. Afraid of me? Really? What and why is she afraid of me? I have no power over her. She is my boss, so she has the power. The truth is hard to hide. That's where all the fears stemmed.

There were six paragraphs of complaints (I will go in detail later). I had answers for all six, only one being a half truth and the other, a hearsay? So I explained anything I could, and the rest I just shrugged and said, "Who talks like that? Not me."

I then went into what I was dealing with all year, and my bosses' boss said, "Why did you not tell one of us?" I said I did. Brainard then looked at Sunny, and she said she was aware. Remember, I sent her a detailed email and told her what had happened right after I asked if she could call me so we could talk. She never called me back. No email. He called it all a catfight, and he wanted no part of it. Looked at me and said to keep quiet during meetings, say nothing, and he asked Sunny to put this all behind us. I only wished that were true. She said, "Will do," but our relationship was strained. Again, in front of people, she talked to me; otherwise, nothing. I spoke only when asked and did things in writing to protect myself. Thus, the diary you are reading right now.

This was a horrific experience. Anna was the one taking notes that day at the meeting. It was said, "Well, this is in writing."

My reply was, "Just because it is in writing doesn't make it true." Those words were as true as its storyteller, just like a computer is as good as its technician. If Anna came to that meeting and they heard both sides at the same time, the truth would have won. I am sure of it. I was never written up officially; I rebutted each paragraph and had it put in my employee file. The ironic thing is, I even got a raise. Go figure.

So now, here is an in-depth explanation on how it went down. It was summer, and we took the children for long walks around trails near a forest preserve. We were always gone about an hour. When we got back, there was an envelope on the counter with my name on it.

After class, I opened it. It was from Sunny, and she stated we needed to talk, that she felt there was negativity in my behavior. "Oh great," I told JL. She asked me if I wanted her to come, and I said no. I would deal with whatever it was and clear the air. Remember, she got back from maternity leave in the spring, and she knew about the behavior of Anna. I sent her an email. I was anxious but thought this could be good to clear the air and tell two sides to any story she may have heard. It was also after the meeting where she told the senior teachers who they would split up. I called her, left her a message, and told her I would be there after class.

When I came to her office, it was dark, no Anna, too, and then I saw Brainard and Sunny sitting in the boardroom. Uh-oh, that was not a good sign. Usually when the two were together, it meant someone's getting fired. Yikes!

I came in, said hi, and was asked to sit down. Sunny showed me a two-page letter of complaints or more like it, hearsays, from Anna. I read it and asked Sunny, "Where is Anna?"

"She did not need to be here" was the answer from Sunny.

"I beg to differ," I said. "Many of these accusations are from her."

Brainard took over and said, "Let's go over each one and you can explain."

Paragraph 1

This was about Lea being in charge of the three-year-old program., and they knew there was negativity about it, so she assumed it was me. This was because it was discussed at that June meeting that she knew there was a problem with it. All I said was, "If all the teachers would have known ahead of time, all the rumors could have been nipped."

"Mrs. Boyes, just stay quiet, will you please."

Mary was the one who was extremely upset that Lea was in charge, not me. They talked about it every time we got together, but I was not going to say that. We had lunch with many of the teachers, and it was brought up, but because it was not mentioned by management officially that teachers were upset. Again, I did not know Lea at the time. JL and I really had no say so as to who was capable and who wasn't. We were not at the facility where she worked. Mary was. We did not know Lea well enough. Because I made the comment about knowing ahead of time, she assumed it was me. That was far from the truth, but I was not going to sacrifice Mary.

I said it was not me. "Because I did not know her or teach with her, I had no comment on that subject. How could I say one thing or another to someone I did not even know?" That was my reply.

Paragraph 2

Sunny said she was splitting up teachers, and I slapped the table and said, "You can't do that!" I was so taken back from that I blurted, "No, that it was Joan who slapped the table [she was two seats from me on my side], and I did not say that." She did. In fact, I talked to her and asked her if she did that, and she said yes, she was tired of all the changes. She even said she would go in and tell Sunny it was her, but then Sunny would know I talked about my meeting, and it could be grounds of termination. (Joan left before the new school year started.) "If I would have slapped the table and spoke to Sunny in that manner, I should have been terminated on the spot," that was my reply. My face might have shown I was not happy, so was JL's, but I would never have said that to a boss at a meeting in front of fifteen people. If I had a problem, I went directly to my boss and talked about it. Always. That was the way I dealt with good and bad issues. I looked at Brainard and told him he should ask all the teachers to come in and ask them one by one if I did such a thing. He said that would not be necessary.

Paragraph 3

The air cleaner issue (more on this later). I told Brainard that human resource came in and okayed it. I thought that was a done deal. Obviously not. It was said I was hiding it from them. The air cleaner was in clear view on the end of a counter we rarely used. If it was hidden, it would not do its purpose. Then it was said that I said I was sad that JL and I were not working together. That was true, but not disrespectfully. I was sad about it, but we had classes next to each other, and if that was what was decided, then I would deal with it. JL was sad, too, but things change, and we were professional enough to handle the change. What was wrong with saying you are sad about something? If I said something against management, then there was a case to be dealt with. I did not. I would not.

Paragraph 4

This one I did mess up. We were at our first meeting after the last one, and JL and I were joking about sitting next to each other. No one was there except Anna, going in and out of the room, but we both were being very silly, like "I can't sit there," or "You better not sit there." And reflecting on it, it was not appropriate, and even though it was in jest, it was not right. I did apologize for that. We should have known better. Anna had ears like an elephant and liked to twist what she heard to make the other person look bad. We did that all by ourselves that time—both of us, not just me. JL never heard about that at her evaluation. Only me.

Paragraph 5

At one of the camps, it was mentioned by a parent why there was a week break for Fourth of July week. I told her it was always like that so maintenance could do a summer cleaning and many people would miss that week because of the holiday. The parent continued to say that the week break made it harder for her three-year-old to get back into the swing. I agreed with her that we would love it if there was no break for the little ones' sake but understood why the break had to occur. It was always that way and was in the book for reference.

It was written WE want to do the program continuously, but THEY, the preschool, does not. What? Who talks like that? I would never bash the preschool to a parent no matter what I felt. I abode by the rules. I worked for the preschool for twenty-six years. It helped my children to go to college. I have enjoyed working here and would never, never say anything to jeopardize that. No matter what was going on behind the scenes, teachers would always be positive to parents. Always. Us versus them. I have only heard one person use that phrase: ANNA, when talking about one facility of teachers to another. I have no idea where she was that day, hiding that day or behind the door? JL did not see her either, but she had to be there, waiting to hear something that she could change to a disadvantage for me.

Paragraph 6

Sunny wrote that I would call the other facility and ask questions as to how they were doing things there. As if I was checking up on management. Both JL and I would call Mary and El because they were friendly with Anna and heard everything from her. Our meetings were informative to a point, but then things would change. We would not hear about the change until we did something, and Anna would come in and say it was changed. This got old, so we would talk to Mary and El and make sure we were on the same page. Just wanted to do the right thing. Communication was not always there when Sunny was gone. Both JL and I just wanted the correct information, that was it. Wanting to be on the same page, that was all. I said JL felt the same way if you needed to talk to her. They never did.

After my explanation of the six counts, Brainard told me to be quiet at meetings and watch what I would say and that "this is more like a catfight." I told him the story about Anna and her hand gesture and told them both that it was a hard year for communication and the half-truth stories that Anna wrote down were basically slander. My integrity was on the line here. I was a good employee, I worked hard, and I just wanted to do the best job possible. If I was wrong, I apologize. I will not apologize for things I did not say. I am confident enough that if each teacher came in and talked about that meeting or things discussed there, I would have been exonerated.

Brainard looked at Sunny and said that would not be necessary. Sunny packed up, and I told her I hope she believed me because it was important that I knew she believed me. She did not answer but nodded. Our relationship was never the same. She believed what she wanted to believe, and those were Anna's words. I could do nothing about that but try my best, and hopefully, it would shine above the chaotic atmosphere that was hovering around the preschool.

Don't let yourself go

'Cause everybody cries

And everybody hurts sometimes ("Everybody Hurts" by R.E.M.)

41

Chapter 8

Summer Mess

IN OUR MONTHLY meeting, Sunny was now back from maternity leave. Two other teachers who were good friends of Anna told us they asked for the camp and got it. I mentioned that earlier. "Really," said JL, "I thought college students were teaching it." They both said it was presented to them if they wanted it or not. Okay. As far as age, they were both two to three years younger than us. So? How could it be that the camps would be too strenuous for us but not for them? JL sent an email questioning the decision, and it was passed off as Mary and El needed the hours, and the missing link was, Anna already okayed it.

Now it had been just a forest surrounding the preschool. It was becoming a swampland, and we were being sucked in. JL was upset more than me. It was definitely more hours we were losing, but we liked Mary and El, and it wasn't their fault. They just lucked out. It pays who is on your side, right? We did other camps (less hours) but did not complain. Who was listening anyway? We still had each other.

There's battle lines being drawn

Nobody's right if everybody's wrong ("For What It's Worth" by Buffalo Springfield)

Chapter 9

Who and What's Lurking Around Us?

JL AND I were split up, as was one other team that was together for years. Found out later that some teachers complained about Mrs. Boyes and Mrs. JL, hearing how their kids loved them and they couldn't get in their classes and how the parents wanted them as their teachers. Who started all that? Come on, it's a toughie—Anna! Why? That was the question of the day. She loved to stir the pot of discontent and envy—I think anyway. JL and I could never understand the purpose of that gossip. No one ever felt good afterward. We sure didn't. Chaos and confusion do not equal anything good. No one could win with that recipe.

JL wanted to complain, but I told her to stay out of all this craziness and that they would leave her alone. They did, thank goodness, but they came after me. I was blindsided.

The meeting with my two bosses did not work the way they wanted, I guess, so a new weapon was about to be used—a mole, but she was in the room adjacent to mine.

I was supposed to be team teaching with a new teacher, Natalie, who had teaching experience. Without any explanation, management switched Natalie and gave me another new teacher, Victoria. We had a late-summer meeting, and I was introduced to Victoria as my new co-teacher. It so happened I had her son in one of my classes years ago. When we got together, JL noticed I was being watched by

Sunny and Anna. "That's okay," I said, "I'm not worried." WAKE UP, MRS. BOYES, WAKE UP! YOU SHOULD BE WORRIED! Went about our business, and later that week, with two weeks before class, Natalie was moved to another class with Katrina, which was attached to my room. I got Victoria. She had no previous experience as a teacher but was a very nice person and ready to please. Okay, Mrs. Boyes, put the alarm on, but no, I did not even think of it. Katrina and Natalie seemed nice enough, and school was getting closer.

We had a great year together, but Victoria did not trust Katrina. "Do you notice how she watches us set up?"

I told her, "Not really." I was too busy just with my own stuff. But when someone mentions something, you do start to zero in on what they said. I did notice lurking around, asking some questions that Katrina should have known already, but I didn't work with her, so I let it go.

Then Natalie started saying things about Katrina, too, like, "Why does Sunny come in our room and talk to Katrina on the side and not stop in your room?" Again, I was clueless and did not know what was going on and really didn't want to. These were prerequisites to what happened the following year. I should have been paying attention. I should have had my guard up.

When the next school year began, I was working with Katrina in two different facilities. She was nice, but I was a little nervous at first. Then when I got to know her, or thought I did, and I relaxed a little. I liked her, and so did the children. So did Anna and Sunny. Uh-oh! Wake up and smell the coffee, Mrs. Boyes.

Little things should have raised an alarm with her, but duh, those stupid rose-colored glasses didn't help me see correctly sometimes, such as this: I would get to the room a half hour early, which we all were supposed to do, but Katrina had to drop her kids off in the morning, so she would get to school about eighteen minutes early. It did not bother me because she said she would stay fifteen minutes later to clean up. Sunny and Anna agreed to it, and I was onboard. Fine, right? But Katrina would get texts from Anna in the morning, and she would be told to change up what the room setup would be, and I would find out after the fact. Annoying, yes, and there was a phone in the room. Why not call me and tell me, knowing I was there? Simple, right? Not for witches though; it takes a while to make those potions and smokescreens.

Now my mom's words "Kill them with kindness" were in my head, and when Anna would come in, I would say, "I like those changes. Doesn't the room look great?" Side glances would be given to Katrina, but that was okay. I have my magical room with children I love, and they loved both Katrina and me, so anything else was secondary. Lots of prayers for strength were said, and it worked most of the time. What's that saying, oh, yeah, "God helps those who help themselves." How true. You have to stand up for yourself!

Katrina and I had our class meeting at a park nearby for an outdoor day. It was a beautiful day, and I stopped by the preschool to pick up our first aid bag and names and phone numbers for our kids. We said we would meet at 9:10 a.m. that day; the parents were supposed to drop off children at 9:20 a.m. I got there a little after 9:00 a.m. and saw another preschool class there already. They started a half hour before us at another facility.

When I pulled up, Anna was racing to my car. "You're late. We were wondering where you were."

"Late, our class was supposed to meet at 9:20."

Katrina was not there yet. She told me the other class was there at 8:30 a.m., so we should have been there at 9:00 a.m. I pulled out our sign-up sheets, which had the time as 9:20 a.m. arrival. Those sheets were sent to Anna and Sunny over a week ago. "Oh, I don't know how that happened." I do. Miscommunication over and over again, trying to make teachers feel as if it was their fault always. Katrina pulled up, and Anna was as sweet as pie to her.

"What happened?" asked Katrina.

"I don't know," I said. "We are here now. Let's have a fun time." We did. Katie was one of the other teachers, a work friend, and she told me after the children left that Anna was raving on and off that Katrina and I were late, "Where are they?" "I'm going to call them." etc. Never got a call. Who's crazy? Not me, not yet.

She's come undun

She didn't know what she was headed for

And what I found what she was headed for

It was too late ("Undun" by The Guess Who)

Chapter 10

Talk of the Town

THIS EPISODE REALLY threw me for a loop. Have you ever felt like you were watching what was going on outside yourself? Here is a good example of that.

In our boss's office was the Xerox machine, and we needed to go there about once a week to make copies of this and that throughout the year. Usually, the teachers would go together, the teams, and make an assembly line of sorts. This time, I was alone, never thinking much about it since I had little paperwork to do. Office was empty, so I started to make copies, and Anna popped in and did small talk as I was wanting to get out sooner than later. From the side, I see two other managers from another department coming outside the room giggling and making siren noises like *rrrooom, rrrrm*, like a police siren. Those were Andy and Joanie, who I had known for years. Andy was actually my boss for a while, some years back, and we were friendly, at least I thought we were.

Coming in the room, they asked, giggling, "Do you need any help? Are you okay? Over and over." I was confused at what was going on, but Anna turned red in the face and would not look at them. They asked Anna again, "Are you okay?" And she said yes but would not look up.

I said, "What's going on?"

They said they just were goofing around and wanting to know if Anna needed help.

"With what?" I asked. Anna looked up and shooed them away with her hand.

"Oh, it's nothing," said Anna, but it was very awkward and strange. I left soon after, and as I left, Joanie and Andy went into Anna's office, and I saw them glance at me, smirking. Then it hit me. They knew about my meeting with Sunny and Brainard and what I had said about Anna and the backhand, dismissing me. They knew about a private meeting between me and my bosses! That was the only thing that made sense to this madness. I was shocked, mad, but sad somehow that now slander was the new thing I was up against. It was something I did not expect. Where are those rose-colored glasses, dammit! I really needed them now.

The office managers who I once knew for years now looked at me differently. I could feel it in my gut. Some people in the office, too, were polite but short. *Slander*, "the action of making spoken statements damaging a person's reputation." There are always two sides to a story; don't be judgmental if you do not know the whole truth or if it is not your business. *Harassment*, "aggressive pressure or intimidation." That was what that was all about. So sad. Some of those relationships I had, many casual, were changed now. Everything was changing; I had to be strong and hold my head up high. It was getting heavier.

When Anna left, slow but sure, many of them started to be friendlier again. I can forgive, but forgetting was hard. I kept trying but needed to put my efforts and energies elsewhere.

When you're out there without care, yeah I was out of touch

But it wasn't because I didn't know enough

I just knew too much

Does that make me crazy

Does that make you crazy

Does that make me crazy

Possibly ("Crazy" by Gnarls Barkley)

Chapter 11

The Anna, Sunny and Katrina Show

BUT AS THE year went on, Katrina got texted during class time at least four times in two hours, and it was always Anna. We were not supposed to be on our phones unless if it was an emergency. I brought it up at our monthly meetings when was it okay to be on our phones. "Emergency only!" Sunny would say. Other teachers asked what about if it has to do with a boss texting? She glanced at Anna and said those texts can be answered after class. It never changed in our class, however, and the texts kept coming in. I just would ask who it was, and she would say, "Anna again." She would text her back. I wanted to scream but did not and just went on.

Another incident: in the winter, JL had a portable room-air cleaner we would use here and there during cough and flu season, so I asked her if I could use it because we were in an older building. She said sure, so I brought it in our room, and Katrina seemed to be okay about it. I put it on (it was counter size) when class was on. I left it one day. Remember, Katrina stayed fifteen minutes longer than me to make up time. I received an email from Sunny about the air cleaner. She said I needed a doctor's note, that it could explode, that is was noisy (really, you did not even know it was on). I said I showed Anna and she seemed okay. Remember the word *seemed*. Sunny came to class after I left with Anna and said that Kathryn, the human resource manager, needed to come in. That's the story

Katrina told me. I said okay. I said I used it the last two years with JL, and she said, "You must have been hiding it." WHAT! No, I chuckled to myself. I never hid it; had no reason to hide it. That Monday, human resource Kathryn came in and said, "This is it? No problem. Just make sure you turn it off when class is over." No doctor's note, no big deal at all. "There's something in the air tonight, hold on." (Thank you Phil Collins).

That's just the way it is

Some things will never change

That's just the way it is

Ah, but don't you believe them ("The Way It Is"
by Bruce Hornsby)

Chapter 12

Katrina Revealed

SO THE YEAR went on. Our three classes were great! Everything seemed quiet then. Katrina was asking me lots of questions about how I liked Anna and Sunny and how long I was planning to work, weird stuff. After class one day, I asked her why all the questions. She hesitated a moment. She proceeded to tell me she was asked to watch me in the classroom and report back if I was not following certain agendas. I was hurt, shocked, and angry. "All year you have been doing this?" She said she was friends with Anna and thought it could help her get more classes for next year. "What about us and our kids? Did we not form a friendship? Are we not a team?" She said she told her I was doing everything according to protocol. Well, golly, how nice of you. She did not mean to hurt my feelings. She was afraid not to do what she was told. I told her, "If anyone asked me to report the doings of another teacher, I would refuse and tell them to do their own snooping." Only if kids were in danger would I go to my boss because of that teacher, then would I report. Otherwise, NEVER! If I have a problem, I would confront that person and resolve it as nicely as possible. But that's me. I think she was upset about the whole thing too. She apologized, but I was never as friendly as I had been. If there was any trust, it was gone. So hurt. I was pretty sure she reported the whole thing to Anna. Now I was going to feel the wrath I was trying to avoid.

When I had our yearly review, it was mentioned if I would work with Katrina again. I knew this was a setup and said, "I will work with whoever you choose." I knew they asked Katrina the same question, and she said she wanted a different facility closer to her home. She did not want to be in that predicament again. How did I know that? She told me. But I had to move my head quickly like *The Matrix* a couple of times not to get hit with those side glances that Anna and Sunny were throwing each other. Nah, nah, you missed me. You missed me.

You've got a lot of nerve to say you are my friend

When I was down you just stood there grinnin'

You've got a lot of nerve

To say you've got a helping hand

You just want to be on the side that's winnin' *("Positively 4ᵗʰ Street," by Bob Dylan)*

Chapter 13

More on Victoria

WORKED WITH JL that summer with camps and had a ball as usual! Some parents asked why we were not together in a classroom for the fall session, but I kind of went around it saying working and mentoring with newer people with less experience etc. was what was wanted.

We had our summer meeting and was given a mom whose child JL and I had four years ago. She did not have teaching experience. Anna asked me over and over, "She has no experience. Are you okay?"

"Sure," I said. "Victoria is a nice person. I'm sure it will be fine." Well, hallelujah, it was! Victoria was a worker! She came in early, left late, and she had a smile that warmed a room and a crazy laugh. We had two great classes and enjoyed each other's company. She did say she was asked how it was working with me. She would reply, "Couldn't ask for a better teacher." I said, "Flattery will get you everywhere." She laughed.

At the end of the year, we got good write-ups from parents, but I did not get the opportunity to work with her again. Always wished her and her family well! Stayed in touch for a while after that. She did not leave on good terms with the preschool. Management had issues with her supposedly. She deserved to be happy, and from what I heard, she is.

I'm never going to walk away

I'm always going to have your back

And if nothing else, you can always count on that ("Never Gonna Let You Down" by Colbie Caillat)

Chapter 14

All About Anna, Witch Number 2

LET ME TELL you a little history about why she was what she was—my take.

In an earlier time of work with Anna, she talked about her mom and what a dysfunctional family she had. Nothing was ever good enough in her mother's eyes, she would say, but her brother could do no wrong. She went to college and graduated, and her brother never could find his niche and lived at home long after she got married. Her mother passed, and she never would talk about it. I told her about my mom and dad, how they were missed, but she never said anything good or bad.

I had a get-together at my house with some of the teachers, some who were fired, and we promised not to talk about bosses. Unfortunately, one of the teachers told Anna about it, and Anna said she was upset she was not invited. I noticed things changed with me around that time, so I did tell her that some people got together at my house, but because they were fired, I felt it would not be a good idea for her to be there. Anna helped one of the teachers to be dismissed. She said, "I bet you had a field day talking about me and the preschool."

"No," I told her. It would have made our time together strained, considering some teachers were friendly with her. No one wanted to take sides, so we had lots to talk about instead of work. I don't think she believed me though. Like I said, whatever relationship we had changed a year and a half ago.

Also, when I think about it, I told Anna and Sunny about my daughter-in-law being pregnant. Anna's first comment was, "Now you don't have to work. You can babysit. I wish that were me." Side glances were given to each other and a bit of a wink. I told them both I was still planning to work and would help out if need be with the twins. It was awkward. I felt they wanted me gone.

Another time, all the preschool teachers were part-time thirty-five hours max, so we could not receive medical coverage. Only four of us were there long enough to get a pension. It was not much, but a nice perk. Being there the longest, I was one of the four.

That year when Sunny came back from maternity leave, Anna was in her office, and my hours were cut to thirty hours, so I wanted to talk. Sunny said all preschool teachers had hours cut. This was not true. Most of them, yes, but two friends of Anna and Sunny got thirty-five-plus. I played dumb, which I was good at (doesn't take much effort), and asked about hours. Sunny said she would have different one-day classes here and there, and I could pick them up every month or so. Anna said, "Well, you are going to get a pension anyway, right?"

I looked at her and said, "What does that have to do with it?"

Sunny stood up and put her hand on Anna's shoulder, and they looked at each other. Sunny then proceeded to say that Anna didn't mean anything by it. But it was then I realized, she resented the fact I was getting a pension, and my salary was the highest there. Believe me, a preschool teacher's salary did not break the bank. It all started to make more sense. They wanted me out. Underlying jealousies, just like in all fairytales. A bit discriminatory, or "making an unfair or prejudicial distinction between different categories of people on the grounds of race, sex, or age." Age or salary? Take your pick.

By the way, as the year went on, I never got those extra hours that were promised. Surprise!

Getting back to Anna leaving, our organization had a goodbye party for her, and all the teachers were there. I wished her good luck. Her husband got a job in another state. I was happy for her and myself. She got to start over elsewhere, and maybe I got a reprieve. She was staying on for two more weeks to help hire the new pre-school assistant.

I thought that this move might be a good thing, but again, watch what you wish for.

Holding back the years

Thinking of the fear I've had so long

When somebody hears

Listen to the fear that's gone ("Holding Back the Years" by Simply Red)

Chapter 15

Lea and the Threes

LEA WAS THE teacher I was assigned with for the year after Katrina. I did not know her well, knew she worked with her cousin Lee for two years in another facility and was pretty good friends with Anna and Sunny. She was bubbly, had a great smile, and was put in charge of the three-year-old program now that Anna was leaving. Remember, there was some controversy about me not wanting her in charge of the threes—made-up stories with my name attached when it was really Mary who started all the rumors. Water under the bridge.

She was nice enough but acted a bit cautious on our first meeting, but all seemed well. That word *seemed* again. Started getting our room ready. I was now doing three-year-old classes only, so I had extra time. Lea changed her mind a few times on lesson plans and decorating, but she had some good ideas. After a week or so, she confronted me by saying, "I heard you were mad I was put in charge of the three-year-old program."

I said, "What, who said that?"

She said Anna told her I was spreading rumors about her to other teachers. I am not as stupid as I look, but I did know a teacher or two who thought she should not have been given the job. Again, I am not perfect by any means, but I do not tattle on anyone. Help me! I proceeded to tell her I did not know her before all this, have heard of her, knew nothing about her classes, and only worked on lesson plans with her cousin one time. We had different age groups, and we were in different buildings, so how could I bash her? I really did not know her.

Thank God she believed me. I was telling her the truth, but I did not give up the name of the teachers who were spreading rumors. I knew who started it, but what good would it do to throw Mary under the bus? We were going to be a team, and my room and kids, our room, meant we had to be on the same page. And we were. She was a bit ditzy at times, but so was I. She had six kids of her own, was a good worker, and had a good demeanor with the children. We enjoyed our classes and laughed, saying we would not let hearsay get in the way of our work. It worked for a while, but the shadows of darkness were right around the corner.

The funniest thing about Lea was, I would tell her something horrific and how I was dealing with a situation, and she would laugh. Belly laugh. I would try to be serious, but her laugh was infectious. I would be laughing and telling her to be serious for a moment, please. She would apologize but say the look on my face telling her was so unlike me, so devastating, that she had to laugh. I got used to it and would warn her ahead of time. Funny, not so much. She didn't know what devastation I was dealing with. I still have to chuckle when I remember those moments. She did get the best of me in a fun way.

Here comes the bad news, talking this and that

Well give me all you got and don't hold it back

Well I should warn you I'll be just fine

No offense to you, don't waste your time

Because I'm happy ("Happy" by Pharrell Williams)

Chapter 16

Introducing Lehra, Witch Number 3

THE NEW PRESCHOOL assistant manager was Lehra, a petite woman who always dressed lovely. She had been to numerous other preschools as the manager, so lots of experience. The day we first met, I was in the room with Lea getting ready for the year, and Anna introduced her to Lea, who said, "We already met," and then to me.

Lehra said, "I heard about you," and glanced at Anna.

I said, "What did you hear?"

She smiled—not a good smile, kind of like the cat who swallowed the canary and left. Even Lea said, "What was that all about?"

"I don't know," I said, but I thought, *Oh no, doesn't seem again like a good thing.* It sure wasn't.

Our class was a good one, but we had a few challenging boys. We knew their number right away. Little Joe was very active, a young three, and his parents were going through an ugly divorce. Regardless on who had him over the weekend, he would be difficult on Mondays. Lea and I thought he might be sleep deprived, and we were very patient with him for the first two months. We discussed him and his situation with Sunny, and she told us to deal with Lehra. Lehra listened to us after school one day and said she would observe our room. The next week, she came in, and Little Joe was having a pretty good day and said she would come the following week to observe again. She gave us some tips and pretty hard criticisms to both Lea and I, but with all her experience, we took them and applied them. Some worked, some did not.

In November, right after Thanksgiving, we let parents come in and help with the class. Knowing time was creeping up, the beginning of November, we asked her to come in again. She stayed an hour and gave us tips and some harsh criticisms again on how to get the class under control. Remember, when Little Joe was having a bad day, one of us had to be near him to stop him from hitting other children, stop destroying other people's projects or art, etc. It was tasking. We had twenty three-year-olds, and on any given day, someone else can be having a bad day too. Parents were signing up to come in November 30, so I saw Lehra in the hall and asked her to come in. Lea had a call from her daughter's school, so she was out of the room. I told her we needed help with Little Joe and could someone come in and observe him. She told me, "Okay, she would get on it." Well, November 30 came. We called Lehra and left a phone message, "Is someone going to observe today or help? Ellen's mom is coming in."

Day started okay. Ellen's mom was there, and then around snack time, Little Joe got angry. He did not like who he was sitting next to, and before we knew it, juice was scattered on the floor and children were crying. Little Joe was trying to get out of the room. (Doors were locked.) Ellen's mom looked like a deer in headlights. I think Lea and I had the same look. Lea had him on her lap, holding him tight, and he settled down. After class, Ellen's mom asked what was being done about this type of behavior. We told her our bosses were working on it. She called Sunny, and then Sunny called Lehra, and Lehra called both Lea and me in her office. She started yelling at us that Sunny was not aware and that SHE was not aware at how bad the situation got. I proceeded to tell her about our conversation in the hall on November 15 and how she said she was on it. Sunny walked in listening, and Lehra looked right at me and Sunny and said she did not remember our conversation in the hall. How convenient for her. A foxy play, play dumb, a good strategy. I'll have to remember that.

One time in a meeting a few months later, she told all of us that she had trouble remembering things and needed our needs in writing. Wish I would have known that. Lea stated that she saw us talking in the hall that day, but Sunny looked at me and said, "Next time, send an email," and left.

Lehra told me, "I don't think you asked for help."

I was upset at this point and said, "You said you would take care of it."

She shrugged her shoulders, and that was that. We did not get an aide until we came back from winter break.

The school district sent a young man named Nick, hired as an aide, who was wonderful with Little Joe. Our room was under control again and happy. We all were. Little Joe just needed a little guidance through this tough time in such a young boy's life. Parents came in and were happy too. Even Ellen's mom came and was glad for everyone involved. We still had moments with other threes here and there, but it was all good. At least I thought so. Sloughing off, Mrs. Boyes.

There must be some misunderstanding

There must be some kind of mistake

I was waiting in the rain for hours

And you were late ("Misunderstanding" by Genesis)

Chapter 17

The Incident: Pickup and Drop Off

WE WERE IN the basement of the building with senior citizens on the first level. When we would get the children, we would line up between two glass doors and proceed in when time was up. Gave parents twelve-minute leeway. Lehra had her office right above the stairway with a glass window to look out. We would wave to her in the morning, and she would wave back. We had Nick for two months now, and Lea took a day off to go college shopping, so I had a sub, Katie, who was with our preschool for years. I knew her well. We all got the kids from their cars. And were between the two glass doors where we do headcounts right outside the parking lot. I told Katie, "Can you be in the front? I will hold the back, and Nick would have the middle line." She said she would prefer the back, being a sub, so I proceeded to move the line forward.

As we get closer to the stairway, I saw Katie was struggling with one of the girls, Ellen, who was now crying loudly and will not move. Katie was trying to pick her up, but she would not let her. Ellen was now yelling. I told Nick to come to the front of the line, wait for Katie, and I will deal with Ellen. Ellen rushed to me and was sobbing. I told Katie to please move at the end of the line to help Nick go down the stairs. I was carrying Ellen, and I saw two of the boys had gone down the stairs right before Nick. I was coming to the stairs right behind the group, and here came Lehra screaming at me, saying, "Where were you? Two boys went down the stairs in front of an adult?" She was in a tizzy state. I was still carrying Ellen, who was sobbing lightly now, and tried to tell her what happened. She was still yelling all the way to the room, would not even try to listen. Everyone was downstairs outside our room, hanging up coats. Katie tried to explain, but Lehra looked at me and yelled with a condescending tone, "What are you doing about this?"

I said in self-defense, "I have a class to teach, and I will talk to you after if that is okay."

Nick was saying, "Why is she yelling at you? You could hear her down the stairs."

I told him I would talk to her after class. I was a bit rattled, but Katie said she would come with me. Class was fine. We went to her room after, and she proceeded to yell at Katie, "What were you doing? blah, blah," when I said, "I will take all the responsibility for the situation." She then calmed down, but if looks could kill, I would not be here today. Katie thought it all went well, but I knew this was not the end of it. I hate being right.

The next day, I received at email from Sunny to come to her office after class. *Dum dum dum dum dum!* I thought I was ready, but when you know you were up against dragons and demons, being right was not enough.

Katie was still subbing, and Nick even wanted to go to the meeting with me, but I said no, it will be what it will be. But maybe if they hear what happened from me, they would see the light. Rose-colored glasses again! Mrs. Boyes, take them off already!

I knocked on Sunny's door, and she opened it, and in the room was human resource manager, Kathryn. No Lehra. I sat down, and Kathryn said she had heard what happened and wanted to hear my side. I said there really was no "my side," just the truth. So I continued explaining how Katie wanted to bring the kids in from the back, me in the front, and Nick in the middle. Ellen had a meltdown, and Katie was having trouble containing her, and with the doors opening to the parking lot, I felt it was an emergency situation for safety. I asked Nick to be at the head and wait for Katie to come and then proceed down the stairs to our room. I opened the second glass door and took Ellen, who was in full distress, kicking and screaming and crying, and told Katie to go to the line of children and help Nick. When I knelt down with Ellen, she was sobbing, poor thing. Remember, she was only three years old. I picked her up and saw the line going downstairs and Lehra running up to Katie yelling, "What are you doing! Where is Mrs. Boyes!"

I told her, "Here I am," with Ellen still sobbing slightly.

"Where were you? You left the children unattended!"

As we were walking down the stairs, I tried explaining what had happened, and she was yelling—yes, yelling, (some people in the hallway looked uncomfortable and put their heads down, but not as uncomfortable as me). I actually was embarrassed for both of us. I tried to explain, with Ellen still in my arms, head buried in my neck. I don't think she even heard what I had to say. I did not say this, but she was out of control. Like my mom would say, "She had a conniption fit."

When we got to the room and everybody was washing hands and hanging up coats, Lehra was still being condescending and talking loudly in front of the class. I told her, "Can we do this after class?" She said yes and stormed out. Nick and Katie were shocked and asked why she was so angry. I told them we would talk about it after class. It took everything in my being to get it together, but I did again. The children put you in a fantasy land that I loved, and the day ended on a good note.

I told Sunny and Kathryn that Katie and I went to Lehra's office right after class and explained what happened (full story). She only viewed the children going down the stairs and me coming fifteen seconds later. Sunny and Kathryn listened and said, "Did you take full responsibility for what happened?" I said yes. Sunny proceeded to tell me I would not be working on Friday and not getting paid for having children's safety at stake. I told them all points were under control except for Ellen, so I picked Ellen as a priority at that exact moment and had Nick and Katie take the rest. She did not agree with two children going down the stairs before Nick, but they were in his sight the whole time. I told her we did the best we could under these circumstances. I also asked, "Where's Lehra so we could say what each other felt or saw or did not see? Communicate. Talk it out."

"She did not have to be here. She told me everything that happened and said you were taking full responsibility. It is in writing," said Sunny.

"True," I said, "but if she saw the whole situation from the glass window, why did she not help Nick on the stairs?" Kathryn shrugged her shoulders and looked at Sunny as if I made a point.

Sunny said, "It's enough information for me. We are done here. See you on Monday." She added, "This will not be discussed again." I got up and cried all the way home. I sincerely felt I had the best interest of my class and would have done what I did again if need be. Just wanted some support. Katie was called in, and she said exactly what I said, the truth. She said that they both had their minds made up already. I never heard about it again until summer when I had my review. What happened to "never be discussed again"?

Nick sent them a written statement on the events of that day but never received a reply. He was let go two months later, with a letter stating, "Little Joe no longer needs an aide." He still could have used an aide till the end of school, which was two months after his dismissal. Katie left the preschool at the end of the school year because of the incident too. Got together with her on and off for about a year. Great person, she just felt that management would not have her back if she needed it. A shame, she was a good teacher.

Let it go, let it go

I am one with the wind and sky

You'll never see me cry

Here I stand and here I stay

Let the storm rage on ("Let It Go" by Idina Menzel)

Chapter 18

All About Katie

KATIE WAS ALMOST too sweet, too nice of a person/teacher. I had worked with her on and off for quite a few years only through subbing. She would call JL and I from time to time and ask about what we did for discipline or how we dealt with kids being picked up at end of the day.

At that time, we had parents come in and get their child by tapping them on the head. One of the teachers would be at the door, and one would be sitting at the circle with them, making sure no left the room unintended. It worked, and she proceeded to tell us that she had done her class with Anna being the substitute that day, and the child got between her and the door and ran in the hallway. She would call the child's name, and they would go in the hallway where all the parents congregated. Of course, this would happen with Anna being there, right? And she got reprimanded by a write-up. She was extremely upset about this, so she asked our opinion on what worked for us. Somehow, she must have told someone else, and the story got back to Anna. Anna came in our room one day and made sure we knew what happened and how it was not her fault but Katie's. JL said, "No teacher wants that situation to happen. It really is not our business." Anna went on putting Katie under the bus, but we went about our business and pretty much ignored her. Was she looking for us to nail Katie? Both JL and I felt very strongly not to get involved in hearsay. I wish others would feel that way, at least our bosses. It would prevent a lot of hurt feelings. Who would think things like this would be prevalent in a preschool setting?

Never mentioned that conversation to Katie. She left after two years, but we would see her for lunch now and again. She said she missed working with kids and some of the teachers, but not any of the management. The preschool's loss. She had the demeanor and kindness all parents want for their child.

Young people speaking their minds

Are getting' so much resistance from behind ("For What It's Worth" by Buffalo Springfield)

Chapter 19

When It Rains, It Pours

IT WAS NOW spring, and we had a very rainy period. So rainy the streets and river were flooding in certain areas. They called for more rain in the next two days, and teachers were asking if school would be canceled. Lehra told all of us that if it was, we would get a phone call or email early morning.

Lea lived blocks away from the preschool, and I was an eight-minute drive. She called me in the morning and asked if I heard anything. I said, "No, we left a voicemail on Lehra's phone but heard nothing." Lea said the river was cresting and the streets were a little flooded already. This was at 7:30 a.m., and we needed to be at school at 8:30 a.m. She tried to reach one of the other teachers in the other classroom and left a message. I said I was leaving now and that I do not know how the streets would be. Well, the eight-minute drive took forty-five minutes with viaducts flooded here and there. Got there, and parking lot was filling up. Got into our room, and it was a ghost town; only maintenance was there. He told us he thought building was going to be closed, so we called Lehra three times. She called back on our phone in the room and was short. "Of course there is no school. The streets are flooding." Lea asked why we were not told, and she said we were the next in line to be called. It was 8:40 a.m. She knew we would be there. School started in twenty minutes.

The next day, we talked to the teachers in the other room. They were called at seven forty-five that morning. Lea then started to talk to Sunny about miscommunications and was told, "If you have any issues, talk to Lehra."

We had an open house at another facility at night to show parents our curriculum and new facility with lots of outdoor activities. One teacher from every room was there, so I was representing the threes from our building. Lehra spoke to the parents, answered questions, and gave examples of how our preschool worked. Some of the teachers knew things were not great with management there for me, but I kept a lot—a lot, an enormous amount inside—and spoke to only JL.

Since the "incident," that was how Sunny presented it. I laid low, was having a good end of the year with Lea and our kids. Lehra started talking about how she came into the threes' room and saw Mrs. Boyes interacting with boys measuring things with rulers. She proceeded to say the boys started using them as weapons (like most boys do) and how Mrs. Boyes took a deadly incident and started measuring the boys with "How many rulers are you?" and before you knew it, the children were getting into a line to be "measured with rulers."

"That's how we like to teach around here—making a negative into a positive." I was floored! What, I did something good? Just like a child wanting to get recognition, I leapt for joy inside. Maybe she did like me, maybe everything was okay. ROSE-COLORED GLASSES! They followed me everywhere, even at night!

We all walked out together, and Lehra was behind me with nobody else around. I waited for her and said it was a good turnout. She said yes, and I started to say, "Thank you for the nice comment about me." I told her I did not know she was even in our room that day.

She looked straight ahead and said, "I call it as I see it" and walked faster to be with some of the teachers she was friendly with. I stood there for a moment, looked up at the sky, and said, "God, help me." Now I get it. It was all for show. Perception.

Lea and I had a great end of the year party with parents and children—singing songs, acting out finger plays, and with a potluck from everyone (we could do that then). After this and that, it ended on a high note, or so I thought. As I said before, working with children is a blessing. It definitely is the most rewarding job on earth. Behind the scenes was a different story.

I didn't care if you hung around me

I didn't care if you went away

All I need is a miracle ("All I Need Is a Miracle"
by Mike and the Mechanics)

Chapter 20

Evaluation Day

TIME FOR EVALUATIONS. Yeah, I was a bit nervous. Come on, Nonie, be honest. Did not have much contact with Sunny, so yeah, anxious. After this year with Lehra, I was frightened, scared out of my wits, really. I knew it couldn't be good. Just didn't think it would be as bad as it was.

I came into Sunny's office with Lehra there too. Started off with, "How did you feel your year went?" etc. Talked about Lea and how we bonded and how little Joe grew as the year went on and how I enjoyed taking some classes that were beneficial to the classroom. They listened and proceeded with how it was an average year for me, taking in "the incident" *dum dum dum dum dum*! I defended myself by the write-ups from parents that were positive and all the positive feedback orally from parents and children.

Lehra showed how she rated me on my classroom skills. She liked my lesson plans, how I played with the children, the control of the class, and my enthusiasm. On the other hand, I was rated average on patience with distressed children (she hardly came in and watched our class, how would she know?). That was rated highly with the parents who were helpers in the classroom. Average rating on "utilizes positive reinforcement with children." She herself rated me highly with the rulers in our class and told all the parents how I turned a bad situation into a good, so what… How can I get a higher rating on control of a class and not that? Lots of holes there. No consistency.

Average on "presents good public image," but I greeted everyone positively every day, according to the parent write-ups, and the write-ups were positive. I told her I did not agree. The worst one, which was not that important but proves a point, was my attendance. She rated average. Really? I had not taken a day off in three years. I was proud of that because I had a good work ethic, and that showed. I thought, *Anyway, goes to show you how you can be perceived a whole different way if someone has power over you and may not like you.* I understand about the not liking part, but sometimes, you have to give credit where credit is due, the facts. They eventually will get caught up in their own web. You can't hide the truth forever. It has a way of coming out—sometimes when you least expect it.

The room was getting darker and darker, and the air was thick as if smoke filled the room. I could hardly breathe. With the two witches together, their spells were stronger than me. *It was only anxiety and their words cutting like a knife*, I thought to myself. Get a grip, Mrs. Boyes.

Lehra spoke first, saying, "Because of the incident (remember, the children going down the stairs in front of Nick and Katie coming in and then me with Ellen crying), we decided that you will not be doing preschool classes but early childhood classes for this next year." They both knew how much I loved my classes and the preschool, and I could feel my eyes filling up and a lump in my throat.

Sunny put her hand on mine. Yikes! Sunny continued and said, "We fully understand if you do not want to continue working here."

That's when God stepped in, and I pulled my hand away slowly and said, "I will work in whatever capacity you want me because I love the children and teaching so much." I wish I had a camera because the look of horror that was on both of their faces as they tried to process what I had said was worth ALL the feelings I was feeling. I had control, at least for the moment.

Lehra said stuttering, "OK then. Anything else, Sunny?"

Sunny had zoned out and came back saying, "No, that's it."

I walked out with my head up but my heart broken. Again, I cried in the car, but I promised myself I will be the last one standing here. One witch down, two to go! This was some dark fairy tale all right! The sun was shining. I put on those rose-colored glasses, and everything was okay. I would be just fine.

There are people in your life who've come and gone

They let you down

You know they hurt your pride

You better put it all behind you 'cause life goes on

You keep carryin' all that anger

It'll eat you up inside ("The Heart of the Matter" by Don Henley)

Chapter 21

Do I Stay, or Do I Go?

I AM SURE you are thinking, *Is she crazy? Is she a masochist? Does she feel the need to be persecuted?* No, no, no, on the contrary, I am just a stubborn person who feels the need to fight for what is right; a true Libra who believes you need to balance everything in life—fairness, the good and the bad; a person who really believes that in good versus evil, good wins. I truly believe that in my life. I try to teach that to my kids and husband, that there is a lot of evil in the world, but just as positive wipes out negative in math, so it is in life. There is darkness all around at times, especially now with the coronavirus at hand, but if we do what we are supposed to and remain positive and believe—yes, believe it with all our being—we will prevail, maybe become better for it. We can do anything if we are all in. I'm in for the long haul.

But enough of that topic for right now. The topic at hand is why I would stay at a place where I was being watched, bullied before bullying was a movement, and talked down to.

I had been there for twenty-six years, was getting a very nice salary (I was the highest paid due to the amount of years I was there), and would get a pension when I left to build upon. I was sixty years old, planning to retire in two years anyway. I loved the families I had gotten to know. Remember, I am also stubborn to the point of "they are not going to drive me out" or "they will have to fire me," and there are no legitimate reasons to do that, so I was looking through the tunnel, seeking the light of the future. I would see glimpses of that light and keep telling myself I could do it. I needed bigger rose-colored glasses for this ride. Don't worry, in my fantasy world, I had plenty of spares just waiting for me. They were always there when I truly needed them. Plus, I had my song lyrics to listen to and get me through. They did just that.

You gotta be bad you gotta be bold

You gotta be wiser you gotta be hard

You gotta be tough you gotta be stronger

You gotta be cool you gotta be calm

You gotta stay together

All I know is love will save the day ("You Gotta Be" by Des'ree)

Chapter 22

Continuing the Adventure: My Support Systems

JL WAS AND is one of my greatest friends. She was so quiet when we first met but became quirkier and quirkier each year with humor that I totally understood. She had two children near the same age as mine and then had her daughter, Hallie, who I had in a gymnastic class years earlier before she got a job at the preschool. What a sweetie! It was great to see her grow to become a wonderful teacher. JL's mom lived out of town and would come into our class to visit and observe. She was very proud of JL, and she should be. We would all go out for lunch, which was very enjoyable. Margaret was and is a great person with lots of wisdom and charm, an absolute pleasure to be with. JL's husband, George, was a nice man with a lot of wit. We had them all at our home before Hallie got married and moved away, and everyone got along great.

It was like we were work soul mates. We never had to tell the other what needed to be done; we just knew what was needed and did it. No jealousies, just camaraderie. We had as much fun as the children, and it showed. Could not have asked to work with a better person. I referred to her as my better half.

When things turned dark, she asked me what she could do. I told her it would be best not to get involved because they would turn on her in a second. She needed her job too. When they gave me the write-up, Sunny told me that if I would tell anyone, I would be terminated and so could the people involved. I did not want that for anyone, me included, so I would vent with her, and she would listen and help me get through it with some suggestions. I knew she felt all the hurt I did, and she gave me tips on how to rise up. Thank you, JL.

I had JL and two other teachers, who I will talk about later, who had taught with me over the years, and they would listen to me and build me up consistently. My sister Mar, who always thought I was from another planet but still always believed in me, was always there for me in whatever capacity that was needed. Huge. My friends from high school—Sharon, Bogie, Diane, Pat, and Gloria—had ears as big as elephants and hearts to match. Three of them were teachers with unions and could not believe what was happening. They were always there in mind and spirit. Solidarity helped.

As for my husband, Cecil, he was my rock and always has been in our forty-five years of marriage. For our fortieth wedding anniversary, he was going to surprise me with a cruise to England, Ireland, and Scotland. He had talked to JL about it, and she told him to talk to Sunny because I was going to be coming back ten days before classes started, and we had meetings, even early childhood, two weeks prior. I would miss two meetings.

My husband called Sunny and asked to talk to her in person. She was nervous on the phone, and he said, "Could we meet tomorrow?" She said yes. She called JL up and asked her why he would want to talk to her and about what. Remember, this was two weeks after my evaluation going to early childhood classes. JL played dumb and said she had no idea. My husband had talked to her to get Sunny's phone number, so she knew what was up. Great friend.

Cecil went to the office building, and when he arrived, her boss Brainard and Kathryn of human resource were there. No Sunny yet. They were nice to him. He was Italian, had a look on him like maybe expecting an offer they could not refuse. Thinking lawyer, suing, nothing to be afraid of, right? Well, Sunny walked in, going around this large conference desk, not taking her eyes off Cecil. "Are you okay?" my husband asked. She said yes but looked worried and exhausted. "No sleep for the wicked," my mom would say.

My husband started talking about our anniversary and how he knew we were supposed to be there fourteen days ahead but explained he booked this trip months ago as a surprise. Sunny's whole demeanor changed. "Of course." She started to smile. "Of course, for such a milestone, no problem. I will tell Mrs. Boyes it is perfectly fine!"

My husband shook all their hands and thanked them for their time, and when he closed the door, he heard, "Why were we called in?" and shut it. He told me that day what occurred and said he laughed all the way home. It made his day to put them in the hot seat for once. He hated to see and hear what was happening there to me. Now, now, I said, two wrongs don't make a right, but I was extremely happy and grateful for what he did. I also asked my husband if he wanted to borrow a pair of my rose-colored glasses. He gave me the look—you know the look that says *"Not funny, don't go there!"* Being Italian, he could not help himself. Love that man!

Talked to Sunny the following Monday, and she was as sweet as pie. Never had another bad conversation, at least not with her. Yay!

Had an extraordinary time visiting the three countries of my heritage—Scotland, Ireland, and England and Paris too! The towns and cities, history, and the people were a dream come true for me! Cecil enjoyed it too. We got to visit Liverpool, and he is a Beatle groupie! The trip was twelve days, and each day was better than the next. The weather was great too! I was visiting castles twice to thrice a day and churches that were back from the 1600s. I was in heaven.

As we were getting down to our last three days there, that anxiety of what will happen next was creeping in my head. So at St. Patrick's Church in Dublin, I prayed to God, Mary, and St. Patrick to be strong, I did not want anything bad to happen to the two remaining witches. I just wanted to be left alone, not be under the magnifying glass, not be yelled at or bullied, but just do my job the best I could and enjoy the kids. I didn't say anything to anyone about how I was feeling, except in my prayers. Mary and Jesus got an earful every night, but the prayers always helped. Could almost visualize them looking at me and trying to run away, thinking, *Let us get away from her*, but they were always there, listening. They always have been.

I get by with a little help from my friends

Going to try with a little help from my friends
("With a Little Help from My Friends" by Beatles)

You are the love of my life

You are my inspiration

Simple and Duh ("Just You and Me" by Chicago)

PS. My husband and my lyric, who is simple and who is duh?

Got back on a Thursday and sent an email out to Sunny about when to meet and what classes I would be teaching. She said tomorrow would work, so I went in with my heart pounding and asking for strength. She was at her desk. I knocked, came in, and she proceeded to politely say, "How was your trip?" then "Have you spoken to anyone?"

"No, I just got back late afternoon."

She continued saying," I gave my two-week notice. Got a job closer to home with more responsibility."

I was in shock, a good shock, trying to have her words register in my mind and listen at the same time. Not always an easy task for me. I never had a poker face. I said, "Are you happy about all that?"

She said with a strong voice, "Yes! I've been wanting to get out of here for a while."

"Well then, good for you," I replied, still hearing those words, *leaving, leaving.*

I must have looked like a deer in headlights, so she said, "You want your class lists?"

"Yeah, yeah," and she gave me them to me. I had quite a few classes and plenty of hours. I got up, said good luck, and turned to her and said, "Can I give you some words of wisdom my mom gave me for life's moments?" She nodded her head, and it just came to me. "Remember to treat others the way you like to be treated."

She looked a bit puzzled and said, "Thank you." That was the last time I saw her, but in my heart, I was bursting with joy! No one got hurt. All good. Two down, one to go, and I am still standing, yeah, yeah, yeah!

These times are so uncertain

But I think it's about forgiveness, forgiveness
("The Heart of the Matter" by Don Henley)

Chapter 23

Let's Not Forget Sunny and Anna at Their Top Game

BEGINNING OF AUGUST, I went to Sunny's office on the matter of my schedule for fall. We were asked what we wanted (two-plus through pre-K), what facility, and number of hours. This was a little different than usual. It was always number of hours, not facility or age group. That was up to management. In the past though, when we had our summer meeting, it would be brought up casually, and nine times out of ten, they would work with us to make us happy. That was the past. This was the new present, full of surprises and more.

This was when I was working with Lea. I had gotten thirty-plus hours the last six years or so, but now, I received mornings only, which cut my hours by six. Some years were better than others when it came to enrollment, so it was stated that everyone would be cut three to three and a half hours. I was the ONLY one who was cut double. Mary and El actually had twenty-eight hours for two years and got thirty-one this time around. JL got twenty-seven and a half, and others got what they had gotten in previous years. I was saddened and upset, of course, so thought we could have communication on this and clear up any miss findings.

I did not fault anyone on the hours they were given—good for them—but when it was said all hours would be cut for everyone but one team got more, I wanted an explanation. That was all.

So I sat down with Sunny first and asked if she could shed some light on how the schedule went and why I did not receive any afternoon hours. Anna was standing outside the room, which she often did, lurking in the shadows per se, so I said, "Anna, why don't you come in and join us? It's fine with me."

She sat down, and Sunny said with no emotion, "Everyone's hours got cut. I explained that already."

I said, "Not really. Some got more, and some only lost two hours or so. I got cut six. Can you shed some light on this so I can understand?"

They both looked at each other, waiting for the other to speak. Anna then said, "Well, you are still getting a pension, right?" I thought. "What does that have to do with what we are talking about now?" That was when I knew things were talked about that should not have been.

Sunny gave her a look of "Shut up," and I then said, "I worked twenty-five-plus years here, and that is a perk I worked for." (In order to receive or be eligible for a pension being part-time, you had to be vested for ten years and work over a certain number of hours a year. Only four of us preschool teachers were eligible because so many came and went.)

Surprisingly, Sunny agreed with me and said that she would be adding early childhood classes at my facility starting late September because two rooms were open. She then said I would be first in line for a class or two, which would increase my hours to twenty-eight to thirty. It seemed promising to me, so I left there feeling okay—not good, but okay.

School started, and I was working with Lea with the threes and one two-plus program when the memo came out stating Sunny missed the deadline to add any more classes and that it would have to wait till January. She did offer subbing for me in the afternoon, which I only did maybe twice a month, until the end of the year.

Being down hours was stressful because I needed to work so many hours a year for that pension. I made it by five hours. Whew! In January, I did get two extra classes which added four hours on a week, making my total twenty-six a week, plus it was in another facility. I was just happy to get those hours and felt I was begging at this point, but with subbing, it worked out. The other preschool teachers knew I was in a bind and delivered. Thank you, thank you, thank you! Still a lot of nice people there.

May you always be courageous

Stand up right and be strong

May you have a strong foundation

When the winds of change shift ("Forever Young" by Rod Stewart)

Chapter 24

A Horse of a Different Color or Witch?

NOW FOR LEHRA, she was not just a witch, but a dragon at times too. Remember, we are in an adventure in a fantasy world where there still is evil, just in different forms.

School started, and I was in the same preschool building for morning classes doing early childhood math, science, music, and art. In the afternoon, I had one class each day but Friday, so I got to see a lot of my teacher friends. It was a bit awkward at times. They wanted to know why I was doing those classes, and I would say, "This is what was offered to me." During my evaluation when I was told I would be doing early childhood classes only, I was told by Sunny and Lehra not to tell anyone about how it was decided. Many of the teachers were worried about Lehra being the only boss we had, now that Sunny left, but I kept my mouth shut and only told JL about the real deal. She felt bad about not sticking up for me two years ago with Sunny and Anna, but I knew she would have quit her job about all that, and there was no need for both of us to be in this pickle. She was and is a true friend. She was one of the four of us who was getting a pension too. Did not want her to lose anything because of me.

I saw many of the families I knew, with some taking extra classes as supplements for their children. Met new people and was enjoying a different curriculum and learning along the way. I had not been doing early childhood classes for eight years or so. It was different because they were an hour to an hour and a half long, and I was the only teacher with eight children. You had only twenty minutes between classes, so a lot of work to get the next class ready. Many of the early childhood classes were different, so even toys or puzzles would need to be sorted out, not counting different art projects or experiments. I should have been buff for all the running around I did. Didn't think I could move that fast. I loved team teaching, but this was good, too, just different. According to the preschool teachers, however, it was perceived as a demotion. In the eyes of my witches, that was exactly how they wanted me to feel—demoted. Not for JL and I, because we had done both and knew when you were alone with eight children and doing lesson plans by yourself every six weeks or so, there was a lot of devotion there. They just didn't know any better. (Until you walk in someone's shoes, you really don't know how it feels).

Lehra would come in my room before class, ask how things were going, and just like Anna, start to talk about the other teachers. Very unprofessional. I'm not saying I don't like gossip ever, but when someone was talking about another teacher negatively, you can bet your bottom dollar you've been discussed too. I would move around the room, nodding my head or not answering at all. Lehra did not like that either. "I'm talking to you," she would say, and I would blame it on "just getting class ready, really busy," etc. and "getting used to working alone."

One of the teachers told me, "Lehra thinks you think you are better than anybody."

My reply was, "Getting used to working alone, and I really need to focus." Made sense and saved my ass. Did not want to hear things that were not my business and could be turned around and bite me. I was learning the hard way to survive. I had finally woken up.

It was in early November when I came in that morning and saw my room changed. The rug was taken out with some stuffed animals and dolls. I went into the room next door, and the one teacher who was friends with Lehra was there. I said, "Do you know anything about why my room has been changed?"

She looked at the other teacher and said, "Let's go in your room." She told me that the late afternoon class had a child with lice.

"What?" I said, "No one told me." She knew, and another teacher down the hall knew. I said, "Can you stay here while I call Lehra?"

"Sure," they both said, so I called. She answered. Remember, she was in the same building.

I asked, "Is it true that someone had lice?" She said yes. I then said, "Why didn't you let me know? Is it safe in the room?" She did not know exactly if it was cleaned for that and asked how I learned about it.

I had the teacher talk to her, Mary, which she was friendly with, and she began to yell at her, "It was not your business!"

The other teacher gave me the phone, and I said, "What do I do about my class?"

She replied, "Change to the room next door till I come."

The other teacher left. Lehra came in and yelled at me, saying I should have talked to her before I talked to the other teacher. I said, "I think I should have been informed, and this would never have happened."

She said with direct eye contact, "Yes, I should have told you." This was the second time she looked at me that I felt a dagger in my body and a look of pure disgust. Ouch.

Can't find those rose-colored glasses. I thought, *Oh, yeah, I left them in the other room.* I put them on, and life was good again. Whew!

Things were coming along, and holidays getting closer always put me in a good frame of mind. Had wonderful Christmases as a child and adult with lots of festivities and get-togethers. Good family time. It was the time we as teachers would get an invite to our organization's holiday party. I went to it every year, and the food and games were great! Talked to one of the teachers at the other facility and asked if she got one. "They would put it in your room," she said. She just got it, so maybe with me being in two facilities, it got lost or misplaced. Made sense to me, but what do I know, right?

Just got news that they hired a new preschool manager and that she was going to start that week. Supposedly, Lehra went for the spot but lost it to this other woman who had fifteen years of experience, Susie. Lehra was asked to stay on as assistant. Heard she was very upset; she held the fort for fourteen-plus months and was looked over. I can see why, but management must have saw something also. They must have gotten a glimpse of her as a witch like I did—the real Lehra.

Talked to other teachers about the misplaced invite. The party was in one week. They said, "Talk to Lehra. She was training the new boss, Susie." After my class, I went to her office; no one was there. I had to turn in my timesheet the next day, so I decided to go then.

After my class, I saw her in the hallway and asked if she had a minute. She had her coat on but said she had ten minutes or so before she was leaving. I went up there, and we were alone. She was facing me, and I asked, "Just wondering where my invite was for the luncheon. I know I need to reply today."

She looked at me and said, with eyes that turned totally black, "You weren't invited."

"What? What did you say?"

Then suddenly, she became as big as the room, with fire coming out of her mouth and wings ready to pierce the windows. She was looking down at me. Her eyes were black as coal with NO SOUL, and she repeated, "You weren't invited."

I struggled to breathe and look at her. She was a monster in that moment. I said, "I have always been invited. We all have been invited."

She said, "I did not invite early childhood this year."

"Why? What would be the purpose of that?" I asked. She said it was her decision. I said, "Well, that was not right. That was the wrong decision," and left the room feeling the singe from the wrath of evil, pure evil. I cried all the way home.

Trust the one who's been where you are wishing all it was

Was sticks and stones

Those words cut deep but they don't mean you're all alone

And you're not invisible

There's so much more to life than what you're feeling now

Someday you'll look back on all these days

And all this pain is gonna be invisible ("Invisible" by Hunter Hayes)

Chapter 25

A Brewin' Is in the Mix

WHEN I GOT home, my husband was furious at the way I was treated and said I should call the regional manager of the preschool. I started writing a letter, stating all the things that had happened to me there (I took notes throughout the three years) and how this issue broke the camel's back. It took me two hours to write the letter, and when I was done, my phone rang. I did not know the number but picked up anyway. "Hello, Nonie? Yes. This is Suzie B., your new preschool manager, and I heard there was a problem and you were upset today with Lehra. Can you tell me what happened?" I told her I was writing a letter to the regional manager, and she said, "Let's see what I can do. Tell me in your words."

I started telling her about the no invite for the Christmas party, thinking it got lost, and then was told I was not invited. She sounded aghast. "Of course you are invited. I am inviting you. So sorry this happened."

"Me too!" I exclaimed. "But are the other four teachers from early childhood invited too?"

She hesitated, saying, "Well, Lehra made the decision about no early childhood teachers, and it is too late. I am really sorry."

"Not as sorry as I am," I said. "Thank you for the invite, however. But if the other teachers are not invited, I cannot go. It's a principle issue now."

"I understand," Susie said. "But you will get an apology for this from Lehra." I told her it was not necessary and how disappointed I was on how this even occurred. She agreed and said with her being the new preschool manager, all will be invited as usual starting next year. "This will never happen again." She also added, "Please come after the party for cake and cookies with the other preschool teachers. They were meeting in one of the rooms after."

"I like that idea. I will be there." She said she would be there, too, but left all of us teachers together. Classy.

Those next few days, I did not see or hear from Lehra. I was asked by a few of the teachers if I was going to the party. I told them I would meet up for deserts after. No one made a big deal. On the early afternoon of the party, I had to turn in my timesheet, and Lehra's desk was next to Susie's. I walked in the office and Lehra jumped up smiling and said in a nice voice, "Oh, Mrs. Boyes, you are always so prompt." She was very crafty to be nice when others were around. I did not give eye contact to her. I couldn't, not anymore. I handed her my forms and stuck out my hand to Susie stating, "Hi, Susie, we talked on the phone but were not officially introduced. I am Mrs. Boyes." She stood up and smiled genuinely. "So good to meet you. Glad you are here."

"Thank you. Me too," and she went down the stairs with me to the room with desserts. The other teachers were all nice, and we started to talk, small talk. "You okay?" I nodded. I had a nice afternoon. Lehra peeked in once but never came in.

I turned my cheek so many times. I was done being nice. From now on, I would only be polite. Lehra never did apologize to me—duh, no surprise.

The next few months, I tried to have little to no contact with her and went directly to Susie. It worked, and it felt better doing it this way. It got even better when Lehra put in her two weeks' notice!

We had our monthly meeting, and Lehra told everyone the news, which most teachers knew already. She got a new position in a neighboring suburb. As she spoke, she looked at me and said to all, "I think I made the right decision."

Looking right back at her—she was her human self at that point—I said, "Yes, you made the right decision."

Her eyes started to change a little. The room was slightly darker, but she composed herself and replied, "I know I did."

After the meeting, one of the teachers asked me, "Was there something going on between you and Lehra? I saw a look."

"A look?" I questioned. "That was nothing," and I just smiled. Ding-dong, the witch was gone—the wicked witch, the last one! I was still standing. All three were out of my life, and I could breathe again. When I was leaving the building, I looked over my shoulder and saw Lehra in her office looking in my direction. I almost felt I should have said something then and go in there, but I just froze for a moment, looked again, and turned and went out. Could not do it.

Heard from Mary that they would go out for drinks occasionally and that Lehra was very upset for not getting the top position. She said my name came up and Lehra made a face. Lehra was smart enough to know Mary and El did see JL and I often, so she said nothing. That was okay by me. The reign of harassment was over.

But before she left, a little insight on Lehra: She was a sharp dresser and, to the eye, was pleasant to look at. She hid her inner demons well. When we first met, she talked sadly about her kids. "We are not close," she would say. They were both in college and never came home long for breaks. I felt bad for her when other teachers and myself talked about shopping and dinners with our kids. She did not talk highly about her husband either. "Now that the kids are in school, we do not have much in common." Again, I felt bad for her. But as she unraveled herself, you could see this other side of, maybe, mean girl syndrome or worse. I think it might have been a prerequisite for the job title. She would talk about other teachers and how they did this wrong, about her kids and how they did that wrong, and her in-laws and how they were ALWAYS wrong. Something was definitely not right with her. Again, I am no psychologist, but when you are pointing at everyone around you, there are three fingers pointing at you too. Like I said before, we all like some gossip, but when there was a pattern, a pattern of "no one is right but you" or "no one can do it the way you do it" ALL THE TIME or you are tearing people to shreds with your words, it gives you chills with all that negativity and jealousy. That is not normal, whatever normal is.

Let 'em laugh while they can

Let 'em spin

Let 'em scatter in the wind

I've been to the movies

I've seen how it ends

And the joke's on them ("The Joke" by Brandi Carlile)

PS Again, I just wanted to be left to do what I did best, teach and just be with the children. I never wished anything bad for those three, just for them to leave me alone. Now maybe I could get back to business, the business of doing a job I loved without someone watching over my shoulder. Hearing negative comments and constant criticisms could be a thing of the past. Rose-colored glasses again, Mrs. Boyes. The after effects were still there with me—in nightmares, looking over my shoulder, a panic attack here and there.

All those were bad chains of events to break. They were hard habits to break, but Susie made it easier for me. She was sincerely nice and kind. She gave constructive criticisms when need be and pats on the back when need be. It was a nice balance to end my year and a half on a good, positive note.

JL retired a year and a half before me, and I truly missed not seeing her. Most of the teachers were new; only two others were there for fifteen years, and everyone else, three-plus years. A new generation, many were very nice. I was still doing early childhood classes (mornings only) and would sub in the afternoon for the preschool. My grandchildren were a little older, and I had time to babysit here and there too. It worked out well. A nice balance. I was still having old memories haunting me, but I played a lot of inspirational music before my classes and in the car, which really helped. All early childhood classes were invited to all gatherings like years before, it was a nice fit. You almost forget how nice it can be.

What the world needs now is love sweet love

It's the only thing that there's just too little of

No not just for some, but for everyone ("What the World Needs Now" by Jackie DeShannon)

Chapter 26

Oh, Susie Q

I ONLY HAD one run in with Susie, not even a run in per se but an amusing altercation. In my world, those two words fit. My daughter lived in a neighboring state and was pregnant with her first child. I wanted to help her out the first few weeks but was told I could not take off two weeks the first six weeks of class. I then decided, since she was due early October, that I would retire but could I stay on as a sub. Susie was happy to hear that and agreed fullheartedly.

The spring session would be my last, and I would be able to sub after. That was what I thought. Then in the early summer, I subbed for a camp twice, and then in the beginning of August, I subbed for a teacher I knew who tried to get a hold of Susie but could not and called me because I lived close to work. She had gotten a migraine so bad she was vomiting. I said yes. I needed to be there in half hour, so I went. I did the hour class, and the next day, I got a call from Susie. "I took you off the teaching list, and you taught without an employee number, and that was against policy!" She was mad! I told her I subbed in June, but she said I was still on the teacher's list but did not put me on the sub list yet for August and the year ahead. She went on and on; my husband wanted me to hang up because she was starting to yell louder and louder.

I said, "Susie, Susie, you mean I can still get in trouble when I am only a sub? Just trying to help out Ariel because she was so ill."

Susie started to laugh. "Oh, Mrs. Boyes, how do you get into these predicaments?"

"Just good at it, I guess."

She laughed, apologized, and said she would look into the policy and let me know what happened. She did just that and said I was still in the system—no change, no problem. It actually worked out better for me. I got to help my daughter and grandson for six weeks that fall, two days a week. Precious moments.

We remained friendly the year and a half I subbed. What a difference in people. Life should always be that simple.

Blackbird singing in the dead of night

Take these broken wings and learn to fly

All your life

You were only waiting for this moment to arrive
("Blackbird" by The Beatles)

Chapter 27

Stories Without Heart

ONE DAY IN the fall, we had a training in case someone broke into the school, the do's and dont's. Everyone felt it was a great idea because we had four facilities, and those were extremely important to know. We had an off-duty police officer there and went with all different scenarios. He wanted us to actually do one as if someone got into the building. There were probably twenty-five to thirty teachers there, and he told us to bar the doors and sound an alarm. We were in two different rooms that had doors next to each other. Alarm went off, and we were supposed to run out of the room to another and barricade the door. As I was running to the other room, I locked feet with another teacher and fell. My ankle hurt, but I moved quickly. When we got into the boardroom, my ankle was swelling. The other teacher went and got ice, feeling bad about the collision, and I elevated my ankle and leg. The meeting was for hours, and JL got ice for me, too, on and off. Everyone knew what happened, but Lehra and Sunny never asked about it.

At the end of the meeting, the other teacher said, "Can you walk?"

I said, "I don't know," and laughed. Putting weight on it was tough, and it was the size of an orange.

She then said to Sunny and Lehra, "Don't you think Mrs. Boyes needs an accident report?"

"Yes," said Lehra, "it looks quite swollen." Yeah. Sunny said she would get one and that if I needed to take a day off, I needed a doctor's note. She left the room to get a form, and I waited till everyone was gone except Lehra. The tables were eight feet long, and she took the paper and literally threw it in my direction and said, "Fill it out and leave at the front desk." She and Lehra left, never looking back.

I hobbled to the desk. The woman there was very concerned. "Do you need any help?"

I said, "More than you'll ever know," and laughed. I did sprain it, but it was a Friday, and by Monday—with lots of ice and elevating and an ace bandage wrap (my husband was a pro at it)—I was pretty good. Black and blue, but pretty good. The two witches never came in and checked on how I was doing. Not a surprise.

Our preschool room at the one facility was attached to a garage where maintenance trucks would pull in and out. It was where the bathrooms were, and a small hallway came through to our rooms. In the cold of winter, some of the guys would start the trucks up to warm them in the garage with the back end of the truck facing the wall of the bathrooms and hallway.

The smell would be excruciating because of the strong exhaust gases. JL and I complained and talked to the guys with the two trucks, but they in turn talked to their boss. And now my bosses' boss, Brainard, came in our room. "I don't smell anything," he would say. It already dissipated by this time. He was eight minutes away, and when they opened the garage door, it was gone. Our children came in about fifteen minutes after this happening, repeatedly once to twice a week.

A parent came in early one day to talk about her child and asked, "Is that exhaust I smell?" JL and I said a truck had gone by in the back of the building. When we told Brainard about the mom, he finally took care of it. It only happened once or twice after. The power of parents.

When Anna took over for Sunny, we had an incident where the room had a stench of a dead animal. Again, having sinus issues, my sense of smell was to the ridiculous. I really could smell things good or bad unfortunately. This was when I worked with Katrina, and I did not know she was the mole checking up on me. So I called Anna and told her we looked all around the room and closet—a very scary closet, even with the lights on and the corners were at peaks with beams—so deep and high, you could not see anything. She looked at Katrina and said, "Do you smell anything?"

Katrina sheepishly replied, "A little bit, but not bad."

It was so bad it smelled like something was rotting away. I said, "I hope a parent doesn't smell it because that would not be good."

Anna said the maintenance department would come in to check, but they did not come in until the next day. It was horrific, so I opened the window in the closet to help and closed the door. I could still smell it.

The two teachers who had afternoon classes came in, but they were good friends of Anna and said they could smell something too but not too bad. I was not crazy, but it was like opening up a garbage can filled with meat that was standing outside in ninety-degree heat. One of the two teachers said she would ask maintenance to come in at lunchtime. He came in, and after ten minutes up in the corner of the closet deep between the beams, he found a dead rat already decomposing. See, not crazy, just mad.

Lea and her cousin worked together at another facility. We talked casually at meetings, but JL and I never worked with either of them. They were very friendly with Mary and Anna and Sunny too. The reason I am mentioning that is the story that follows.

It was the day after Spring Break, and we were trying to get in the groove, moving a little slower than usual. We had a good day. The children enjoyed being back, and so did we. We were cleaning up our room, which was taking us a little longer than usual, when Anna came in. She asked how our day went and started talking about Lea and her cousin. At first, we did not get what she was getting at, just rambling about how they taught etc. Then she told us that no one showed up for their class. I asked, "No children came today?"

She laughed and said, "No, no teacher was there."

JL said, "What, how can that happen?" It sounded preposterous.

Anna told us that they both were out of town and got subs for that day, but only one sub came and did not have any information on the class, so Anna was called. Anna started to do the class with the sub and left messages with Lea and her cousin. No reply. At the end of class, Lea came in, just got home, and supposedly she got reamed out.

It was very uncomfortable to hear all this. We did not know them very well and with Anna telling the story, not sure where the truth started and the mistruths ended. Both teachers got reprimanded, with one losing one day of pay. That was the rumor going around.

One of the subs did not show and should have been there, but in reality, when you got a sub for your class, the teacher had to send it to the boss to get okayed. Someone dropped the ball or both did, but again, your boss should not discuss anything about another teacher and her class. It was not professional and not moral, just plain wrong. This was when we knew what we were dealing with, and no one was safe.

Anna was looking at us waiting for a response. "What a shame," I said. JL nodded her head. We continued cleaning, and Anna left. Whew, eggshells all over the floor, and we managed not to land on any of them, at least that time.

Then, another time with Lehra and Sunny on at least on two or three occasions after our meetings, I was asked to stay behind to talk to them. It would be an interrogation about what I did in the classroom to make sure it coincided with Lea's version. Lea had no idea they were doing that to me until she waited with me one day after a meeting and did not leave. Anna and Sunny were a bit uncomfortable, but I was used to it, so I said, "What can I do for you ladies?"

Uncomfortably, Lehra asked about our coming end of the year party and what time were we doing it. Lea said, not knowing what is going on, "You just asked me that yesterday." and proceeded to tell them about the time and other details. She just smiled and asked if there was anything else.

"NO," they both replied, but again, if looks could kill, they probably would. Lea was oblivious, which was good.

I told her, "Thanks for staying with me."

"No problem," she replied with eyebrows clenched in puzzlement. Welcome to my world. I needed Botox between my brows with all that puzzlement.

One of the summers, poor JL had an injury that caused her to renege on working our camp. We had planned already, and camp was about to start in less than a week. Many of the teachers took off for the summer, having younger children at home. Lehra was the boss and said she would get a replacement. She did, a college student who was the child of one of her friends. She was going for her masters in education. Candice was nice and seemed to really study me, but I had nothing to hide, so that was okay. JL, I miss you already! She was great with the kids and friendly enough. God only knows what was said. This was after "the incident" with Lehra. It was a six-week class, four days a week in the morning, and we were by trails and parks, which made the time fly. She took off a few days here and there for school, and I got to work with some teachers from the pre-school. Everything seemed fine. Beginning to hate the word *seemed*. It haunted me. When the camp was over, Candice said, "It was fun to work with you." And I wished her good luck. She said something to the effect like, "Good luck. You might need it."

I laughed and said, "We all do sometimes, right?" She shrugged her shoulders and was not smiling. Hmm, what was that all about?

When I had my end of the year evaluation, it was brought up that I would tell children if they were crying, "You're okay, you're okay. What can I do to make you feel better?" Usually this happened at camps more than school because children got hurt playing outside, minor issues, but still needing assistance. Leaving parents on any given day would be hard, and I would say, "Mom or Dad will be back soon," trying to distract them with toys or books. It usually worked.

The only way she knew that was, someone told her who was in the room with me. She never came in the camp's room except after it was over. *It's okay*, I thought, *it was appropriate behavior on my part.* Lehra said I should have said, "Oh, you seem sad. How can I help you?"

"Okay, sounds good, but I have never been told that before," I said. Candice had to be the one who told her what I said. Wouldn't you know it, another mole. Same scenario, different witch. I said, "Did Candice tell you that? Because I don't think you were in the room to observe that." I asked like a deer in headlights. Lehra said it didn't matter who told who, but I replied, "If I would have known, I could have used the right verbiage."

Sunny looked at her like that might have worked, but she continued on saying, "You would take pieces of paper and glue them on art projects for the child. That is not appropriate."

Now, I was starting to lose it inside. I was a big advocate of children doing their own thing. Anyone who worked with me, even when art had to look the same back in the day, I strongly believed it should look like child's art. Period. Their own masterpiece. She started telling a story about a little boy who did not want to finish his art work, and I added pieces to it. Where was that and when? She looked down, and it hit me. At the camp, one little guy, Charlie, did not want to do the art project that day, and when he was putting it on the art rack, I put a pile of paper he cut into small pieces on top of the project held with a paper clip. I told him he could finish when he wanted to at home. Candice was right there when he was putting the art project on the rack and saw me. See what happens when you don't see the whole picture? The ending is the way you want to see it.

I said, "Anyone who worked with me knows how important it is for children to do their own thing. I don't finish art projects for anyone, only encourage children to make it their own. Where are you getting this misinformation?"

Lehra did not look up, so Sunny continued with "Let's move on."

I couldn't win, I knew that, but I had to stick up for myself. Hearsay is exactly that—the report of another person's words by witnessing an incident, which is discarded evidence in a court of law. This was a court of the Mad Hatter in Alice in Wonderland. Mad, crazy mad.

Come on now who do you who do you

Who do you think you are?

Ha ha ha bless your soul

You really think you're in control?

Does that make me crazy?

Does that make you crazy?

Possibly ("Crazy" by Gnarls Barkley)

Chapter 28

Words of Wisdom?

YOU MIGHT BE asking yourself, "Why would you put up with that? Nothing is worth that treatment."

You are right. I am not a martyr by any means, but the classroom and children were my refuge. In the classroom, it was a wonderland of thoughts and dreams and hopes. I did not see any boss for five days or so, maybe two weeks, so it was a reprieve of sorts. I NEVER let it get in the way of my class. My fortress would not allow negative behavior to enter. My class was full of love, life, and hope—again, one of my favorite standbys: *Hope*, a feeling of trust, a belief that something good can happen; its strength is the strength of a person's desire or wish. I live my life hanging onto that feeling!

I had my husband, sister, and friends to vent to when needed. The hardest time was at night; I would have nightmares on and off of people watching me, forgetting something for class, just plain fear—an unpleasant emotion caused by the belief that someone or something is dangerous likely to cause pain, a threat.

My husband had insurance from his job that allowed me to speak to a psychologist once every two weeks for two months on the phone. She was very easy to talk to, and I told her of my situation and how I was doing well overall. She said the dreams or nightmares were my subconscious telling me it was a release of emotions that flooded my subconscious but were definitely real. It is how we try to cope, how a person deals effectively with something difficult, like stress. She knew I did not see them for a week or two at a time, so she gave me some suggestions at how to deal with that time frame—inspirational songs, saying poems, reading a few inspirational books, and knowing I had faith, prayer (was using that one all the time). If I was alone with them for any reason, I'll be nice, but I'll stick up for myself in a positive way. Instead of agreeing with them, say, "I understand," which keeps me in control of the situation. Try being with another teacher when confronted so I have support and backup. Those tidbits of info truly helped me. I felt more empowered and protected, but unfortunately, it did not stop all the nightmares, just lessened them, and I still can have one now and again after eight years here and there. Crazy!

I did what I felt I needed to. Was it right? Maybe not, but I needed to know that good versus evil, good overcomes with persistence. I needed to prove to myself that I would be the last person standing. And I was. They all left, and I still remained, maybe better for it in a weird, distorted way. I sincerely felt I was stronger for it. I took a different approach to them when I realized why people are mean or why people harass or why people bully. I actually started praying for them, feeling that they needed help. I don't really think anyone wants to be mean or bully others. It is because that person is unhappy with themselves or had an unhappy life somewhere down the road, or they witnessed that behavior at home when they were young and vulnerable. I believe we all want to be the better of ourselves, but life throws those curve balls of emotions like hate, jealousy, and power, and we can make the wrong choices. We are all human, except for the three witches, but seriously, we ALL make mistakes. Some we learn from, and some we do not. I wonder if people who act mean to others or bully them, really don't realize what they are doing. Not aware of the severity of their actions. Just plain don't know better? Not an excuse by any means, but what if those actions make them feel better about themselves? So they fall into a bad habit of repeating them over and over again. If that type of behavior makes them feel better about themselves, then they won't think it is a bad thing, right? A bit warped, but it helped me rationalize my situation, and actually, I felt sorry for them that they had to resort to that behavior in their lives. Life is hard enough. Walking the line of sanity, it's not always easy to follow that straight line.

I will now share with you some of the sayings and prayers that helped me be better, that helped me understand, and that gave me strength. Maybe they can help you too.

> Yesterday is history, tomorrow is a mystery and today is a gift. That's why we call it the present. (Eleanor Roosevelt)

> I want to be on your side or your best side, not in terms of some political kingdom or ambition, in love and in justice and in truth, and in commitment of others, so we can make of this old world a new world. (Prayer by Martin Luther King Jr.)

> Be careful whose toes you stand on today. You may have to kiss their feet tomorrow. (Unknown author)

> I expect to pass through life but once. If therefore, there can be any kindness I can show, or any good thing that I can do for a fellow being, let me do it now, and do not defer or neglect it, as I shall not pass this way again. (The Sandbox)

> Love is a positive force. Bullying is negative. If someone tries to bully you, feel the sense of strength you get when you choose to love that person instead of trying to hurt them back. The golden rule tells us to treat others as we want to be treated. Be an example for others. Love has the power to change people, and it empowers you. Don't give anyone the opportunity to make you feel less in any way. Know who you are. Know

your rights. You may not be perfect, but never allow anyone to make you feel inferior. (Donna Fargo)

Give us this day our daily bread and forgive us our trespasses, as we forgive those who trespass against us (So difficult, but if you don't forgive, you can't move forward). ("Our Father")

Gossip is about power and social currency. The person spreading it feels powerful being "in the know". They believe putting down someone else through malicious gossip increases their own social standing. (Amy Dickinson, "Dear Amy" column)

The Eagles song "Heart of the Matter" line "I think it's about, forgiveness, forgiveness, even if you don't love me anymore," all the lyrics from "Somewhere over the Rainbow," all the lyrics from "When You Wish upon a Star" by Jiminy Cricket from the movie *Pinocchio*, and "Don't fret about tomorrow's problems, todays are enough."

Words by Hunter Hayes's song "Invisible"—I would play this over and over before a meeting with my bosses "Oh, and never be afraid of doing something different, dare to be something more / Yeah the words cut deep but they don't mean you are not alone and you're not invisible / There's so much more to life than what you are feeling now/ and someday you'll look back on all these days and all this pain is going to be invisible."

"The Joke" by Brandi Carlile—played this in my room before class if I felt a little weak, to strengthen my will. It helped and still does when I feel melancholy. "They can kick dirt in your face, / dress you down and tell you that your place is in the middle, /they hate to see you shine."

This next song's lyrics helped me when I was angry, and I would listen to it in the car to get out that feeling and feel empowered instead. Tom Petty's lyrics of "I Won't Back Down," "No, I'll stand my ground / won't be turned around / and I'll keep this world from draggin' me down / gonna stand my ground / and I won't back down."

"Be kind. Be kinder" and "Two wrongs don't make a right." This is one of the hardest: "Love your enemies." Also, "Turn the other cheek"—I was ALWAYS rosy, "Keep your friends close, your enemies closer"—I don't want to, and "Nothing is easy."

"Kill them with kindness" is a great one because if someone is kind to you, it's almost impossible to stay mad at them. It stops them in their tracks. They do not know how to react, so they retreat.

"It's a wonderful world if you don't weaken." My mom would tell us that when something wrong or sad happened, rise up over whatever it may be. But my son did some research on that saying, and it has to do with people losing their minds if things don't go their way. (I like my view on it a lot better.) Or "no rest for the wicked," same connotation.

The lyrics from "Instruments of Your Peace," "Where there is hatred we will sow his love / Where there is injury we will never judge. / Where there is sadness we will hear their grief to the millions crying for release."

"You Gotta Be" by Des'ree—I absolutely love these lyrics! When my kids were in high school, we would be in the car, so I had a captured audience. I would sing these words to them, and they would roll their eyes. "Okay, Ma. Ma, that's enough." We would laugh about it if I did not put it on, so I think they got the message. Little did I know that the message still stood out for me those three years "Listen as your day unfolds, / Challenge what the future holds, / try and keep your head up to the sky, / Go ahead release your fears, / Stand up and be counted, / Don't be ashamed to cry."

We love sports, so from Babe Ruth, "You just can't beat the person who never gives up."

But everyday I'm more confused

As the saints turn into sinners

And I feel this empty place inside

So afraid that I've lost my faith

Show me the way

Show me the way

Take me tonight to the river

And wash my illusions away ("Show Me the Way" by Styx)

Chapter 29

Teachers and Friends

WHEN I FIRST started, I did early childhood classes, so basically, I was on my own, except for lesson plans. A group of four of us would get together every six weeks and draw up lesson plans and pick one another's brains on ideas, books, and crafts. There was no Pinterest or internet help, so we would get together at our local library. These teachers were like me, with little children at home, some trying to work fewer hours to go back to school for themselves and teach at the public schools when kids got older.

We had a wonderful time, and each one of them brought something to the table. Creative, fun times, and learning time for all of us.

About Barb

Barb was a preschool teacher for years before she came to our preschool. She taught early childhood classes before she got the assistant job. She was a lot of fun, had an infectious laugh, but a bit feisty. She was a strong person and spoke her mind when needed to. Barb did not work at the preschool when the witches were all there. She worked with Sunny for six months and left. That was when Anna took her job. She always warned me about "Sunny not being your friend," but did I listen? No. I had all these signs coming at me—people getting fired, teachers leaving, things being said, etc. Duh. I'm not a smart man, woman.

Barb had two sons near my children's ages, so we had a lot in common. Her husband was a good man who would plan special vacations for them because she might have mentioned she would like to go to, and he would get the vacation rolling and go! She also enjoyed exercise classes and book club and took very good care of herself.

Barb was a worker. Great work ethic, very organized. The best of times was when she was our assistant. Things at the preschool ran so smooth; no glitches. All the teachers liked her, and the bosses all knew they had someone special.

She needed to move on, and when she left, so many things changed. It goes to show you in life what a difference one person can make. That's Barb.

We would go out for lunch here and there, usually JL and I, but sometimes, other teachers, too—no problems. Life seemed simple then. Oh, oh, the *seemed* word again. I have such a problem with that word. *Seemed*, "give the impression of being something or having a particular quality. Used to make a statement of one's thoughts, feelings or actions less assertive or forceful." I don't like that word. It doesn't work for me. When Barb left, she got out just in time to miss all the evil and darkness that went on behind the scenes. She told me once that if she worked there when all things went amuck, she would have had my back, even if she would have lost her job. I believe she would have too.

About Elizabeth

Elizabeth was a fantastic worker and was organized, very prompt, and always prepared. She had been a grade school teacher back in the day and taught at another preschool for years. She still did. JL and I shared rooms with her, and she did not always like the way we left the easel. Elizabeth would write us notes about how to clean it, etc., and I would like to "pull her a little" by writing notes back, adding flowers and hearts. I don't think she appreciated that very much—my humor was on the silly side, and hers was not. We spoke in person, and I would hug her—JL too—and say we would be neater on that easel. We even started to take the smocks home and wash them. She had a valid point, and in the long run, it made us better at leaving the room as clean as could be. She would laugh and tell us "we needed training," and she was right. Never too old to learn something new.

Elizabeth was ten-plus years older than us, but you would never know it. Her energy level was amazing. Still is today! She loved children, and it showed. She loved science and had wonderful ideas for the classroom. Elizabeth looked great too—always dressed beautifully and did not look or act her age. She became a very good friend. We all still get together when we can. I made friends for life from working at the preschool. Wonderful memories too. Priceless.

It was summer, and Elizabeth did not work weekly camps. She did have one specialty class of science, an evening class. One of the perks from the preschool was, we would get a free ticket to the neighborhood fest if you worked through the summer. Usually, you got it from your boss, but I think we were in between bosses, and I was told to ask a woman named Joanne for tickets. I knew of her, said hi when I was in the office, but never had to deal with her.

I told Elizabeth I would get her a ticket and went after camp. Didn't realize it was trying to climb Mt. Everest, but I went through a series of questions that lasted five minutes, and she had to find "authority" to give me them. I waited another five minutes or so, and she told me they did not usually give another ticket to someone if they were not present. I told her you could call Elizabeth at home, but reluctantly, she gave me both. I dropped off the ticket for her, and she was happy I got it for her. Told her, "You owe me," and we laughed at how guarded the tickets were. I had been there over twenty years, and Elizabeth had been there ten-plus, so they knew us. It was probably just protocol. We ended up seeing each other there and enjoyed a concert with our husbands. Good times.

Lean on me when you're not strong

And I'll be your friend

I'll help you carry on ("Lean on Me" by Bill Withers)

Chapter 30

Not-So Magical Times

THE TIME CAME for JL and I to move forward and join the regular preschool. She had such a hearty laugh and the same dry, quick humor as I. We hit it off from the start, and people came and went. Teams were broken. She had heard there was an opening for team teachers in the adjacent preschool and said, "Let's go for it." I agreed, and for eight-plus years, we were THE TEAM. We were not looking for that title; it just happened that way. We had such good chemistry it really took off in the classroom.

We made good friends with many of the teachers, went out for lunch dates, etc. Two in particular, Mary and El, were our closest. There was Rita, too, who came across a little tough, but you learned to like her. We then met Barb and Elizabeth, and they showed true colors later, still being friends today.

Funny thing about women is, you think things are good and may say more than you should, and it comes back and bites you you-know-where. That was what happened with Mary. She did not intentionally mean to stir the pot, but when it came to talking to Anna, the pot was out of control, making an overflow of "she said, you said," etc. Anna had a good way to get people to talk. I sometimes gave more info out than I should too, at least in the beginning, but I learned not to. I never took anything against Mary. She just trusted her bosses, both Anna and Lehra, and told them things that if you put a little spin on it, you were caught up in a web of lies.

For instance, JL and I worked at one facility, and Mary and El were at another. At meetings with Anna and Sunny, it was stated, "Someone's trying to cause problems here. I don't know who it is, but I will find out."

El looked at me and said, "I don't know of anyone, do you?" I said no, wondering where all this was coming from. JL shrugged her shoulders, and everyone around the room looked scared. We were. Three people got fired between May and August, and we felt like, Who is next on the list?

Little did I know that the incident about the chair that I told Mary and El that summer was somehow in a conversation that "Mrs. Boyes told us about the chair story." So getting back to us being in different facilities, they would call us and check on what we were doing, and we would ask them what they were doing. Simple things like bulletin boards, what papers were due when, etc. Well, Mary told Anna about our calls to them asking what they were doing in their room, probably in a simple conversation like, "Have you talked to anybody? What are they doing in their facility?" So Mary, time and again, would mention the phone calls, not thinking much of them, because there wasn't much to tell.

In Anna's eyes, the common denominator was ME, and because of the meeting where I told Brainard, my bosses' boss, about her yelling at me on the phone and waving her backhand dismissing me, she got reprimanded, I am sure, and now I was the target. I was the one in their eyes causing problems, all because we did not get the communication from the top and all because of a few simple questions to make sure we were doing the right thing in our room. Remember, we were told to do our bulletin boards one way, which we did, and then Anna came and tore it off the wall, leaving it on the floor right before our class started. Communication—most important between employees and boss. Trust. Respect. We were scared at any repercussions, so talking to Mary and El, who were tight with Anna, seemed like our best bet. They had the inside scoop, right? Wrong, because now it looked like JL and I were questioning their authority on what to do with lesson plans, etc. Again, we were scared. We just wanted to do the right thing, whatever that was. Mary did not intend it to sound that way, I know that. A conversation is just a conversation between friends and colleagues until it is misinterpreted by another or how that person wants to hear it. Remember, the game telephone? As a child, the first person whispered a message, and as it went down the line, chances were, that message was something else. That is what I think happened. I did not pick up on that until it was too late. Both JL and I were pretty naive, I guess. Never saw that freight train coming. *Whoo whoo!*

You can stand me up at the gates of hell

But I won't back down

No, I'll stand my ground ("I Won't Back Down" by Tom Petty)

Chapter 31

Being Decent and Humane

AFTER THAT HORRENDOUS meeting with Sunny and Brainard about the six paragraphs of complaints, Brainard thought it was more of a catfight and "keep your mouth shut at meetings, Mrs. Boyes, so you don't get in trouble." Nice support, huh? He added, "Don't ask any questions either so things don't get misconstrued." He was right though. I had to really watch myself.

Well, the next day, JL, El, and I had an extra class to take on music in the classroom. After class, JL told El what had happened to me, and I came and told her the rest. She was flabbergasted at the accusations and the false statements from Anna. I told her to watch her back, and in turn, she told me she would not repeat this even to Mary. She was a good person. I trusted her. She even asked if she could do anything to help, but as I told JL, "No reason for you to get in trouble too." I was told that if I told anyone about what had transpired at that meeting, I would be let go and the other people involved would likely have the same outcome. That answered that.

The music class for teachers was on a Saturday, so back at school on Monday, Anna came in our room and asked how we were doing. I made sure I was busy and did not talk to her much anyway; JL was polite. It was hard for her to do that. Crazy how as adults, you have to play games, but sometimes you have to.

That afternoon when I came home, El called. She was very nice but direct. Anna asked her, "So you did a music class with JL and Mrs. Boyes. How did it go?" with a mischievous smile. She told me she felt Anna was fishing for information. El told her it went fine. "Anything else?" Anna asked.

"No, it all went fine," said El. "Why are you asking?"

"Nothing, nothing," said Anna and left the room. El NEVER told anyone about what I had told her, and we never discussed it again. El was a good person, thank God!

Think of your fellowman

Lend him a helping hand

Put a little love in your heart ("Put a Little Love in Your Heart" by Jackie DeShannon)

Chapter 32

Input on the Preschool Teachers

THERE WAS ANOTHER teacher who did both early childhood classes and preschool classes. Her name was Ariel. Ariel was a bit like Eeyore from *Winnie the Pooh*. It was her nickname, and she would laugh about it. The sky was always falling, and the walls were crashing down, but seriously, she did have a complicated life. Her husband died young—in his late forties, about five years ago—and she had some money problems. She did not work at the preschool at that time, but the hurt was real. All the teachers felt sad about her situation.

Ariel also lived with her son and his family, so she felt she did not have the independence that she wanted so badly. She was a very nice lady, extremely likeable and very chatty and a little out-there. I could easily relate to that. One day after my class, she came in and asked if I had a minute. She proceeded to tell me that Anna was asking questions like "Have you ever worked with Mrs. Boyes? What kind of teacher do you think she is?" This all happened after that meeting with Sunny and Brainard too.

I said, "So what did you say?"

She said that she said, "Yes, I have worked with her and thought she was great with the kids and had a good class." She also said that she thought I was a good teacher. She then informed me that it was said, "Really, are you sure?" Ariel then said, "What is going on with you and her?"

Remember, I could not say anything to anyone, so I said, "I don't know, but I will find out." I did know already, but that didn't make it any easier to hear from another teacher that your boss was talking behind your back. This was a crossroad for me. I had to put it all behind me and move forward or leave. I chose to stay. After that, if someone questioned me about our bosses or why I was not talking about them when everyone else was (women can get catty sometimes), it was my decision to stay away from the negativity. If someone started talking about them, I would walk away, be busy, and choose not to listen because it did not help me at all. This was what I needed to do to survive. And I did. Sometimes, however, it was said, "Oh you think you are better than us? Come on, Mrs. Boyes, you have an opinion too." I would say, "I do, but another time." Not their fault. They didn't know what was going on. I had to watch everything I said, even if I felt others felt the same as myself. My armor was on. I could only take it off at home. I shrugged my shoulders. Another time was now.

Mrs. V was one of the sweetest teachers I ever knew. She kept her mouth closed, said very little at meetings, had health issues, but worked through them. She also lost her husband at an early age. Very sad. I subbed in a few of her classes, and she subbed for JL so we worked together quite a few times and enjoyed one another's company. The children loved her too. What a nice demeanor. I still talk to her from time to time. Her grandchildren were in my classes at different times. Enjoyed them too. She was a very good lady.

I mentioned Rita before. She worked with Mrs. V in the classroom next to ours. Like I said, she was not easy to figure out at first, but once you got to know her, she was likeable. She had a more structured class than ours, but it worked. On Fridays before class started, we would get together and have coffee and donuts and chitchat. This was before I had any issues, but she was having some with Sunny and Anna and would tell us things. Both JL and I would think she was exaggerating. Why did I not prepare myself or have eyes in the back of my head? She was eventually one of the three who were fired.

Rita went into Sunny's office, but she was not there. It was the end of the school year, and she was asked to come in and do her review early. She had another job for the summer. Anna was there and said Sunny was running late and was extremely friendly to her. That should have been a clue as to what was about to transpire, but again, when you were not a witch, you didn't think the worst, right? In came Sunny, Anna left smiling, and in five minutes, Rita was terminated. The grounds: insubordination. Rita asked on what grounds and was told a parent said she said something derogatory about the preschool management. "Can you tell me who and what I said?"

"No, it has already been decided, and if you protest this, we will not give you unemployment benefits, so what's your answer?"

Rita took the deal. She did still get her pension from them, but a lot less, since she was thinking she would be working another seven years. She was so taken aback. She worked two jobs and needed it, so there was no other choice. Preschool teachers do not make a whole bunch, but the ones who do it love those little rascals. The joy of the children makes up for the monetary amount. Such a shame we did not have a union or anyone—except human resource, who almost always sided with management—to help us teachers. It's a preschool for Pete's sake. Can't we just get along?

Spoke to Rita maybe three or four times after that. She was still livid about being railroaded, questioning if she made the right decision. I questioned myself that same feeling for three years on and off, but everyone must do what is best for them. Rita found another preschool closer to her home and did work those seven years there. She did what she had to do, and so did I, whatever worked. I never let her know what happened to me or that I was the next in line for the sharpened ax or poison apple. Going through that crazy behavior—boss is nice, boss is mean, another boss is worse—and hearing about that bring up old wounds that you wish to forget. You should learn from what you see and hear. I wasn't prepared for what was coming, but I should have been. Little by little, I learned the hard way. I always was a little slow, but my pace was about to accelerate. Hang on, Mrs. Boyes! It was going to be a roller-coaster ride. I hate roller coasters!

When people can be so cold?

They'll hurt you, yes, and desert you

And take your soul if you let them

*Oh, but don't you let them ("You Got a Friend"
James Taylor)*

Chapter 33

Info on the "Other" Management

KATHRYN WAS THE human resource manager. She would always say hi when we would run into her, which was not often until the three witches came to the palace. In those three-plus years, she was at five different meetings with me and whoever the boss was at the time—maybe six times with the coming to our room on the air cleaner event. She was a very pleasant person, a great listener, but she would bring a pen and paper pad with her, and it made me uncomfortable, at least at first. I told her once after three other meetings, "Should I be bringing paper and a pen too?" Remember, I was taking notes, and JL, too, through the course of those years just in case I needed backup.

She replied, "Oh, no, I will put it away. No need for you either."

Okay, I thought, *we would just talk, and she would listen to my take on whatever the "problem" was*. I felt I was very open and honest with each meeting, because I thought the truth would set me free. Most of the time yes, and sometimes no, but I did not get written up except that one time when Anna did not come to the meeting with Sunny and Brainard but had six accusations written. Kathryn told me if I did not agree with those accusations, which I did not, I could send a rebuttal, which I did. When I signed the paper, I also wrote Do Not Agree, which Kathryn said was my right also. For that, I was very appreciative.

One of the last times she came to a meeting was with Lehra. Lehra was trying to explain herself as to why I did not get an extra class for the last semester of early childhood. It was a lame excuse—so and so needed more hours, too, and I subbed more frequently blah, blah, so she gave it to the other teacher. Kathryn asked how I felt, if that was a good explanation, and I said no. I told her that Lehra promised more hours after the holiday directly to me, but of course, she could not remember doing that. Lehra either had a memory loss issue or playing dumb was her best friend. I think I know which one it was. Nevertheless, Kathryn did not have much to go on and sided with Lehra, telling her if anything else came available, to give it to me. Lehra smiled and glanced at me with an SOS message on her forehead in caps saying, "AIN'T GONNA HAPPEN." Did Kathryn not see it? I saw it as clear as day. Sometimes I wished I did not see or hear the things I did. Kathryn said she was going to lunch, so I said, "Maybe we should go to lunch one time. I feel we have gotten to know each other so much better these last few years," and laughed. She did too. Lehra did not. Now the SOS message was on my forehead, "HELP ME." No one saw it or cared.

About Brainard

When I first started at the preschool with very limited hours, Brainard just graduated from college and was in charge of the IT department, if they even called it that at that time. It was the late eighties. He was a clean-cut guy with a nice friendly smile. You just knew he was going to move up the ladder if he stayed. And he did. He got promoted three times and became my boss's boss, Sunny at the time. In fact, he was one position higher than that. He did well for himself. I was happy for him. I think he was well liked by everyone, and he dealt with all these women around him quite well.

He did not like any problems though, and knowing me somewhat all these years, I think when Sunny, Brainard, and I had that meeting, it was uncomfortable for him. He did not like to be the bad guy (who does?), but sometimes, you have to settle things before they get out of control. Brainard only put out that one fire, at least he thought he did, by saying we needed to get along and for me to be quieter at meetings so I would not be misconstrued. That fire never got extinguished though, and the enchanted forest surrounding the preschool was catching fires on and off for three years. I should have gone to him later, but I did not. My fault. If ever those situations get out of hand, go to the higher-up boss. Trying to deal with those witches and all their powers was too much for me. I could have used his help, but I wonder if he thought all was well. I'll never know. He did not like confrontation, that I know, but I should have given him a chance. He was not the bad guy here. He was just clueless. My bad. Learn from my mistake. Help is out there if you look hard enough.

Well I know what's right

I got just one life

In a world that keeps on pushin' me around

But I'll stand my ground

And I won't back down ("I Won't Back Down" by Tom Petty)

Chapter 34

Funny Stories in the Classroom: From the Mouths of Babes

BACK IN THE day, we used to bring in food items and make treats with the children. That was a great time to use math skills in measuring or how many cups do we need, etc. tablespoon or teaspoon, what is a quarter cup and half cup. Even the three-year-olds were very interested, but the five-year-olds asked a lot of questions and made the most comments. They had stories about their moms not letting them do the measuring because the measuring cup was too heavy, "Don't make a mess," "Keep the flour on the table please," and "Get your hands out of the bowl." It's funny, at school, I did not mind the mess as much, and believe me, it would take us double the time to clean having eighteen five-year-olds no matter how good they were. They were all so serious about it, which would just make you smile. Then the end product, whether it be a cake, a cookie, or a drink of some sort, the excitement rang in the room. They were so proud of themselves, rightfully so.

One day, JL and I decided to make a hot chocolate drink with all the trimmings—sprinkles, whipped cream, marshmallows. We just had to do it at the end of class because the children would be sugared up, and then they could go home and bounce off the sides of the car. We always gave the parents a heads-up, and they would laugh. The ride home had to be something. We would do this once a month usually with whatever theme we had going or letter of the month.

It was in February we decided on the hot chocolate. What child does not like that? They measured the milk, added two to four teaspoons of chocolate powder, and even let us know how long they wanted it in the microwave. Many wanted warm chocolate. Then they added any topping they wanted, one teaspoon each, and some looked like little mountains with very little liquid. They all seemed to be enjoying their masterpieces, except for Jack, who had a very sad face. "What's wrong Jack?" I asked. "Did you try it?'

"Yes, Mrs. Boyes, but it's not Café Mocha from Starbucks!" He put his face in his hands very dramatically. Both JL and I had to look away at first. It was so cute. We were smiling but did not want him to see.

"I know It's not Café Mocha from Starbucks, but you made this drink. You should be proud of yourself."

He took his hands off his face and said, "Okay, but I don't have to drink it, do I?" Again we had to look away and told him he did not have to drink it, and he was smiling.

After class, we took his mom off to the side and told her the story. She was laughing so hard and said, "Oh no, I developed a Starbucks junkie, and he's only five!"

JL and I had show-and-tell in one of our classes. It was the first time that year. We usually would do it after the children were in school for three months or so, so they would feel more comfortable talking to the group. Each week, we would have three children bring in something that meant a lot to them. Some needed coaching to talk; others would go on and on, adding "and, and, then," etc. as if it was one sentence. Adorable! It was a great tool for speaking in a group and building self-esteem. Stuffed animals, toys, books were the most popular. One day, we had James to be the show-and-tell person, and he went into his book bag and pulled out a pamphlet. It was about a credit union. He then proceeded to explain what a credit union was, all the things it offered, hours, etc. I learned something that day. James was so serious and went on and on and was very enthusiastic in his delivery. After about five minutes, one child raised his hand and asked, "What is a credit union?" James was ready to talk again, but we stopped him and thanked him for all the info. Again, we had to turn away so he could not see us smiling. He was like a little executive. Priceless. We asked his mom if his dad worked there, she said no, but how some children like to go to McDonald's, James liked to collect papers, slips, and envelopes at the credit union. And she laughed and shrugged her shoulders. We would wonder if James became a president of a credit union or owned one as an adult. Who's laughing now?

At the preschool, we would have entertainment come in about every three months, such as music, science, and dancing. It would last about forty-five minutes, and the children loved it. We did too. This time, it was when Anna was in charge and things were a bit iffy. We were told a gentleman was coming in with banjo playing music and games about farm animals. She could never remember the gentleman's name, and we dared not ask too many questions because of the wrath afterward. After many questions from the children, of who was coming to sing, I told them he was Barnyard Pete. Anna told us it was two words, so JL and I thought Barnyard Pete was as good as any. Well, the gentleman came in and introduced himself as Bob the Barnyard Man. One child who was sitting in front of me turned around and said, "Where is Barnyard Pete?" JL heard that and started to laugh.

I just said, "Oh, this is his brother."

"Okay," he said and shrugged his shoulders. It worked, no questions asked. Everyone enjoyed the music, and we laughed about that story for years.

We started to do more dramatic play in the classroom, which JL and I loved. So did the children. Every two months or so, we would have a section of the classroom set up as a doctor's office, grocery store, fire station, library, etc. We both felt it was a great learning tool of everyday life, and boys and girls enjoyed doing it.

One month, we decided to do a veterinarian's office with stuffed animals and all medical supplies with dress-up clothes. The children loved it because many had animals at home, and the ones who did not, wished they did. Children learned how to take turns being the doctor or nurse, waiting in the waiting room with their animals, and being the cashier. It was fun to watch. It was time to clean up, and once we did, we went to play outside. We had a castle out there and an opening at the top, which most children would "be the king of the castle." This day, Dillon went to the top right away and, with one of the stuffed animals and his stethoscope yelled, "I am the best vegetarian in the world!" We talk about that story, too, and laugh. So sweet, so innocent. That's why it is one of the best jobs in the world.

It was winter, and the weather was exceptionally cold, so we could not go out very often. Right outside the window was our court-yard covered in snow, but it was too cold to play. JL and I noticed on the eaves of the building were giant icicles. We were doing a lot of science experiments and talked about maybe getting a few and teaching about solids versus liquids, melting items, etc.

The one afternoon we decided to get a few icicles, it was getting above 32 degrees, and some of the icicles were dripping. Remember, science was not my forte, but I am not stupid, or at least JL and I thought not. I went outside with all the children, and JL was watching through the window. The windows were older, so the kids would yell out, "Get that one, Mrs. Boyes! Get that one, no not that one," etc. Now a smart person would realize you cannot tug at icicles because they are attached and not only will the one you want come down but the whole thing would come down. Again, not thinking clearly, I pulled down on the largest one. The children were cheering. It was about two feet long, with one-foot icicles clinging to it. Boom! It came down all right, right on the top of my head on the right side. I felt a little woozy, but I had the mambajamba in my hand. The children and Mrs. JL were laughing at first, but then one of the children said, "Mrs. Boyes is bleeding."

I came in, and sure enough, I had a little blood trickling down my face on the right side. It didn't hurt, but it was startling. All the children came around me and helped me with an ice pack. They asked Mrs. JL if I needed a Band-Aid and got the first aid kit. JL asked if I was okay, and I was laughing saying, "I think so." We got that icicle in a pan, and it took one hour and thirty-six minutes to totally melt! The children were so attentive and concerned, holding my hand and sitting on me and next to me. It was so sweet that they were so concerned. They acted as if they were the adults and I was the child. Pretty much after that, we all learned it was not so smart of a stunt. When the parents came to pick them up, they all told the story about what happened and how brave Mrs. Boyes was. I can think of a lot of other adjectives and adverbs to describe my actions. The children learned a lesson that day: Do not pull on icicles and stand under them, be with a responsible adult, and be smart and use a broom to knock them down. I learned it the hard way. Ouch!

Did not fill out an accident report, but I should have. Again, Anna was acting boss and did not want any added ammunition to my list. Funny thing was, six months later, I had issues of vertigo when I would go from a lying to sitting position. Went to the ear, nose, and throat doctor, and he asked if I had a blow to the head recently, and I said no. Then he asked if I had a blow to the head within the last six months. I really had to think hard because I thought I did not. Yes, I did, the icicle experiment that went bad. He put me in a chair, tilted it back and forth, side to side. Had me lie down and get up. Dizziness gone! Amazing. He told me about three stones you have on a ledge of some sort in your ear for equilibrium. If those stones fall off that ledge, they float around in your ear, giving you vertigo sensations. With him turning my head this way and that, the bones go out of the ear and are absorbed by the body. I guess you don't really need them. Crazy! I learned a lot from that experiment, and it never happened again. Thank you, Dr. Lee.

It was the end of the year, and we would celebrate summer birthdays our last two weeks. These were our five-year-olds, and they were pretty clever, starting to add and, of course, recognizing their numbers. Circle time was the time to have the birthday person to stand up, tell us when their birthday was or going to be, what kind of cake they wanted, etc. One little boy, Carm, told us all about his birthday and then proceeded to tell us about his sister's birthday and Mom and Dad. He told everyone how old his mom and dad were and turned to me and asked how old I was. I said I had a seven and a five in my age. One other boy, Thomas, yelled at us, "Mrs. Boyes, are you seventy-five!"

I laughed and said, "No, I am not that old yet. I feel like it sometimes.

Carm, as serious as can be, said, "No, silly, she's fifty-seven."

One of the other girls said, "That's old."

Again, from the mouth of babes, reality hit. JL and I laughed about that for years. How we both wished to be fifty-seven again.

What the world needs now is love, sweet love

It's the only thing that there's just too little of

What the world needs now is love, sweet love

No not just for some oh but just for every, every

Everyone ("What the World Needs Now" by Jackie DeShannon)

Chapter 35

Amusing Stories at All the Facilities

JL AND I had an afternoon early childhood class with fifteen children. It was an hour-and-a half class once a week similar to the preschool class, helping parents with children getting ready for kindergarten, getting used to being away from Mom and Dad. One boy, cannot remember his name, never was away from his family. If they needed a babysitter, Grandma would babysit. This was not unusual for many families, but this class was a nice taste of what school would be like.

She warned us that when he would get upset, he would put his fingers down his throat and throw up. One tidbit about myself: I had a real bad gag reflex. I could handle anything else, but that was a toughie for me. Of course, I did not tell her about it; we would try as best as we could to prevent that from happening. Poor JL. She knew she would be the one watching over him because otherwise, she would have us both out of control.

The first week went okay. We distracted him enough times that when his mom came in, he and she were very happy. The problem was, once they knew the schedule, the second time around was usually the hardest. We had a few criers, a little better the second week, but this poor little guy must have tried five times or more to vomit. He was afraid and nervous. Each week, we thought it would get better, but by the fourth week, he did throw up in the garbage can. We had to call the mom; she changed his clothes and wanted him back into the class. We let him in again, and the mom waited outside the waiting room. She said she would bring something that would help for next week. *Good*, we thought, *something from home that would get him to feel more comfortable.*

The next week came, and the mom brought in a paper bag. "Oh, did you bring in something to help console your son?" asked JL. "Stuffed animal, toy, blanket, or trinket?"

"No," she said, "some black garbage bags that he can carry and 'catch' himself." We were not too pleased at that, but believe it or not, he never vomited again. Whatever works, right?

Most of our buildings were old—forty-plus years and things would go haywire. There was one time JL and I smelled gas-type odor that would come up from the bathroom sewer now and then. Usually, the maintenance would pour water down it, and the smell would dissipate. Called our boss, and she called maintenance, and someone would come that morning. It was decided we would be outside all day for the morning class, and we did just that. Thank goodness the weather was warm, and the children thought it was super cool. Talking about it, we were lucky we smelled it and kept the children away. Don't know if it was dangerous or not, but they worked on it all day. When parents picked up, the children all said we had class outside. We replied, "It was a last-minute thing," of course, not mentioning what really happened. Sometimes, we were left to our own devices. Not always good.

In another facility, we were on a public golf course. It was a separate building from the small clubhouse, but we would lock the doors as instructed, and men would come and bang on the door from time to time wondering why the door was locked. Probably nobody ever was there before, thinking this was the clubhouse. Some of the looks from these golfers were from astonishment to frustration. JL and I would have to go the door and explain that this was a class for children and to please go to the next building. We would not open the door but talk through the glass. Finally, after two months of this, a sign was put on the building and an arrow for the clubhouse. It still happened, but less frequently. When we brought this up at a meeting, it was said, "Oh, just deal with it." That was exactly what we did.

Another time, it was winter, and of course, the golf area was closed. It snowed about six inches the night before, but roads were okay for driving. Didn't even think about the parking lot until I looked and tried to get in. It was not plowed! Called my boss, Andy, and told her I could not get in and had a class in forty-five minutes. She apologized and said she forgot about my facility. She called someone, and they came ten minutes later and plowed the parking lot. I had a shovel in my car for emergencies, so I shoveled the walk to the building as the guy finished the lot. I was soaking wet from sweat and got the room ready, and the parents and children came in. This was a class with parents. Brought some snow in a pan so they could color it with old markers. It really worked well, and the children loved it. The parents loved the idea. Someone asked if we were going to play in the snow today. My answer, "I already did." The parents laughed because I had my shoes on a mat that was filled with snow.

"It looks like you did," they said and smiled.

I sang to the shovel, "You're all I need to get by" after class. Another day, another adventure.

At the same facility, JL and I plus two other teachers—Elizabeth, our friend, being one of them—had early childhood classes in the morning. Elizabeth had told us she had seen mouse droppings here and there and informed our boss, Marie, about it. Maintenance came and did whatever they needed to do, and all seemed okay. One day, JL was doing a class by herself and getting supplies out of the cabinets. She opened one closest to the door and screamed. A little field mouse was sitting, looking right at her. She called Marie and was told not open that door until maintenance came. Poor JL, she had to do the class knowing what was in the cabinet. Her fear of the mouse was like how I felt about the subject, vomiting. She made it, however, and maintenance took care of it. At a meeting, it was brought up, and many people laughed about it. JL did not. I understood, but we did what we had to do. We were warriors in preschool clothing. Every day was an adventure.

This story happened to JL alone. She had an early childhood class in the afternoon in a different room. It was a dreary day, and we needed the lights on, even in our class that morning. David was not there that day, so Marvin, who did other things for the preschool, was on duty. We saw him in the morning, a friendly man who would always sigh before he spoke. It was his trademark.

We cleaned up our room, and I left, but JL was on her way upstairs to her afternoon class. It was really dark in the hallways, and when she came to the room, there were no lights on. JL turned on the lights and screamed, "MARVIN!" Poor Marvin was lying on the mats in the corner, taking a little siesta. It was probably his lunchtime, and he did not realize anyone would be coming in. JL apologized for screaming. She did not expect to see him lying there and was wondering if he was okay. He jumped up startled and apologized, and they both started to uncontrollably laugh. "You scared me," they both said at the same time. Funny story, they kept it to themselves until he found another job. Then JL told me, and we were always careful what was behind the door. I had been doing that for two years already for different reasons.

Laugh laugh I thought I died

It seemed so funny to me ("Laugh Laugh" by
The Beau Brummels)

Chapter 36

Crazy, Fun Times

IT WAS HALLOWEEN time, and we could all get dressed up if we wanted. Some teachers would just wear jeans and a flannel shirt, which was fine, but JL and I loved costumes. This one year in particular, we decided to go to the hilt, and I went to the Salvation Army store and bought two pink '80s prom dresses. They were perfect, with puffy sleeves and some sparkle; we were going to be beautiful princesses. We even got tiaras and magic wands to boot.

We were laughing so hard at ourselves—two late-middle-aged women, finally after all these years, to be princesses. When we opened our classroom door, I wish we would have had a camera to see the expressions on the parents' faces. From horror to surprise to complete "Are you serious?" we saw it all in those thirty seconds. We were just having fun, and the children loved seeing us that way. They were using our wands, calling us Princess Boyes and Princess JL, and wearing our tiaras. It was the best Halloween ever. JL has our picture on her phone to this day. You only live once, so live it to the fullest. We always did in our magical room; nothing could touch us there. The memories are priceless.

I took it another step farther. My brother in law, Bob, was in the hospital again. He was with my sister Mar. I came to his room with my princess outfit, but he was not there. Here they came around the corner, and the look was, "What the—!" My sister was laughing so hard, and Bob was chuckling, shaking his head. They could not believe I came dressed like that. The staff thought I was a singing telegram or something like that, but Bob said, "No, that's just my sister in law," and laughed. I sprinkled fairy dust on him to help him feel better. My sister said it really brightened his spirits. He deserved any laughter he could find, any levity at all. He was an amazing guy. No problem for me, princess or not, anytime.

On Fridays, JL and I would play some dancing music for the fours and fives class. They loved it, and so did we. Good exercise for sure. We played "Fade-away" by the The BoDeans, which was one of the children's favorites. We would get a little wild, but everyone chimed in. On Fridays we had our coffee mornings, and even though I asked for decaf, many times I would get caffeine instead, which made me hyper than usual. JL would tell the other teachers, "Oh no, it's going to be one of those days." And it would be. Caffeine and I were not very compatible because I would have too much energy at first and then feel tired after that. Or it could have been all the dancing, too, that made me so tired. Duh.

We would play "Wizards in Winter" by Trans-Siberian Orchestra and dance, then freeze, then dance, then freeze when the music hesitated for five minutes straight. We would dance and laugh and feel aches and pains after. That was one of the children's favorites too. We did that for the parents after class one day because they talked about it at home and wanted to see what they were talking about. Better watch what you wish for, right? The parents watched and probably were astonished that those two fifty plus-year-old babes could still move, or they were thinking, *Oh please don't continue*, but we did anyway. We laughed about their faces on that and the princess outfits. Unfortunately, that was the same year, and they probably thought, *We are leaving our children in THEIR hands?* The magic of preschool. What happens in a preschool class stays in a preschool class. Ha!

Now it was David's turn—the best maintenance man ever! What a wonderful guy. He was retired but with a work ethic beyond belief. If JL and I asked him for ANYTHING, he was there lickety-split. All the teachers liked him. We would tell his boss and ours about how well a job he did, no matter how large or small.

He would come in about twice a week and just talk about what he was doing on a weekend, etc. David had a group of college friends who loved car racing, and they would all go down and see the Daytona 500 every year. Everyone lived all over the United States, but everyone would come, rain or shine. He was a very interesting person and a kind one too. One morning he came in and showed us pictures of the race and his friends. Good stories, guy stories but ones you liked to hear. He also showed us pictures one of his friends had with what to do with duct tape. Remember, this was before YouTube and Google, so JL and I were amazed. One picture was a small engine plane with one of the wings torn off. The short video showed how they used duct tape, and the plane flew a short distance and landed safely. We were impressed! If anything broke in the room, like a table or back of a chair, we would call David the Duct Tape Man. He was like a superhero, and many times, it worked well enough till we got a replacement.

We did not realize that David, too, had to watch what he said. We had a grocery store setup for dramatic play, and Sunny called to tell us to clean it up and that it was not David's job. We never asked David to clean it up. When we would leave our room, it was tidy, a lot tidier than my house.

The next day, we talked to David and said we were sorry if we left the dramatic play area messy and he felt he had to clean it. He laughed, shook his head, and said, "I told Anna, when I moved the one table, boxes fell down, and I had to clean it up. I was not complaining at all, it was just a conversation in passing." We smiled and told him we fully understood. He said he would watch his words next time. We all had a good laugh.

Later that year, a similar story. We asked Anna if David could move one of our bookcases we were using for dramatic play. Anna told us that David did not like going back and forth to our every whim. Okay, but now the bookcase needed to be nailed because one of the shelves was loose. We waited for David to come into the room, and he looked at it. He said it needed another screw and came back five minutes later. Again, we apologized and said we had heard from Anna stating he did not like going back and forth to the facilities. Being the man he was, he said, "I never said that. Anna said I should not be going back and forth to different facilities. I told her that's my job to help each facility with whatever it needs." Discrepancies even with maintenance. David, what a guy.

David had to run to three different buildings for the preschool and early childhood classes. He would clean the rooms, set them up for us, and even bring supplies that were heavy. Every preschool room was different in size and setup, and we all gave him a run for his money. Not deliberately, but we really made him work, and he would tease us but never complain.

It was near the end of the year, and JL and I did an overhaul of our room for spring. We had a different dramatic play area, a flower shop, and needed furniture moved around. David shook his head smiling and did all that we asked for. Every year, we would get him a gift certificate at Bass Pro Shops or Starbucks, just to thank him for all that he did. He was very appreciative, but honestly, it was not enough. We should have done more. He was that special.

We had our end-of-the-year party with parents, too, and after the party, David came in and asked how it all went. "Great!" we exclaimed, and he handed us an envelope.

"What is this for?" we both asked.

"Just open it," David said with an impish smile. Inside was a certificate stating, "Number 1 preschool team for changing their setup of their room more than any other." He got us good that time. We laughed about that, even apologized, but he said that it was all in fun. He stayed and ate lunch with us (lots of leftovers from the party).

David was a remarkable man, and he retired the next year. All the teacher's pitched in, and we got him a large-sum gift certificate, card, and a chocolate chip cookie that fed an army. He got teary eyed and thanked us. David got lots of hugs that day. We thanked him, too, and told him he would be sorely missed. He was one of a kind.

Oh I get by with a little help from my friends

Mm going to try with a little help from my friends

Yes, I get by with a little help from my friends

A little help from my friends ("I Get by with a Little Help from Our Friends" by The Beatles)

Chapter 37

It's a Wrap

MANY, MANY, WONDERFUL people were at the preschool. Many were loved and missed. Each person touched my life in one way or another, mostly good. Fond memories of families and children, teachers, and bosses. Overall, it was a great ride. Even with the three witches, I still learned from them. They might have been hard lessons to learn, but to survive, I had to dig deep to understand them. No one likes confrontations or losing battles in life. I don't believe I lost anything. I believe I gained understanding, strength, and fortitude. Sounds deep, maybe too rosy, but that's the only way I choose to look at it.

It took me seven-plus years to write this diary or even look at my notes. Reading them would make me relive those moments. Many times, it was too hard to bear. That is why I put it in a more magical or storybook-like setting. Once I started writing this, it was therapeutic. Like closing a door or finishing a chapter of a book you don't really like, the end product was not as bad as it seemed. The good outweighed the bad, and that is how I feel about life itself. Taught my own children that not all things will go the way they want, not everyone will be their friend no matter how hard they try, but their attitude toward whatever comes their way will be what saves you.

You can't change things, but you can change your attitude toward them. Need to tell myself that over and over some days, but it is so true. Be true to yourself, and you can't go wrong. No could have, should have, would have, you can never go back—only full speed ahead. No big regrets; hopefully you learn from them and no longer get caught up in them again. You need to turn the page to move forward. I am moving forward, totally forward now. The story has been told; the message is clear.

A man can tell a thousand lies

I've learned my lesson well

Hope I live to tell the secrets I have learned

Till then it will burn inside of me ("Live to Tell"
by Madonna)

Always be yourself, be respectful, but don't let anyone make you feel small or invisible. Never. If this happens at work, hopefully, there is someone who can help you resolve it. I chose to stay, and I dealt with it through the support of friends, my husband, and sister and prayer. What is good for one person is not necessarily what is good for you. That is something you have to weigh or balance yourself. But you are never alone. Remember that: NEVER ALONE! Slander, harassment, and bullying at any age, at any time are always wrong!

The three witches left, but they also left a heavy trail of malice behind. Through all my support systems, I made it through with very little scars. It took about eight years for me to open my diary, read the notes, and tell the story that needed to be told. One day if they ever decided to go down that dark road again, maybe they would be stopped and would have to pay the consequences. Maybe they learned from my journey, who knows? I sincerely hope so. People can change at any age if they look in the mirror, really look and they do not like what they see. They can put a stop to that type of behavior and be the person they would want to be, the person they used to be or dreamed to be. Unfortunately, they had to witness that type of behavior sometime in their life. They learned it the hard way, even if they did not want to learn it. We do as we see sometimes. Sometimes we fight within ourselves and promise never to repeat that act again. Second chances. Reflection of our lives are all things that can turn us around at one time or another. As people, we have choices in everything we do. We don't always make the right ones, but if we learn from our mistakes and not keep making them, no one loses. It's a win-win situation.

So no more secrets, no more lies, no more keeping it inside. Thank you, Madonna.

I hope you learned something from my diary and laughed a bit too. I am grateful to have written it and have learned to deal with all those emotions and feelings, which can still haunt me from time to time. Time for me to listen to my own words: turn the page for good, keep the humor, and move on. Sigh of relief and joy. Keep on truckin', Mrs. Boyes, a whole lot of living to do. Two song lyrics to wrap this up; Sir Elton and Barbra say it best.

PS The names have been changed to protect the innocent and the guilty.

You know I'm still standing better than I ever did

Looking like a true survivor, feeling like a little kid

I'm still standing after all this time ("I'm Still Standing" by Elton John)

There's a place for us

Someday

Somewhere

We'll find a new way of living

We'll find there's a way of forgiving

Somewhere ("Somewhere (There's a Place for Us)" by Barbra Streisand)

A Whole New Chapter Begins

Bibliography

Ciccone, Madonna, singer-songwriter, and Patrick Leonard, song-writer. "Live to Tell." Track 4 on *True Blue*. Sire/Warner Brothers. Released in 1986.

Hart, Corey. "Never Surrender." Track 3 on *Boy in the Box*. EMI Records. Released in 1985.

Williams, Pharrell. "Happy." Track 4 on *Despicable Me 2 Soundtrack*. Sony/ATV Music. Released in 2013.

Streisand, Barbra, singer, Jule Styne, and B. Merrill, songwriters. "People." Track 12 on *People*. Columbia Records. Released in 1964.

Adkins, Adele, singer-songwriter, and G. Kurstin, songwriter. "Hello." Track 1 on *25*. Sony/ATV Music, XL Recording. Released in 2013.

Jules, Gary, singer, and Roland Orzabal, songwriter. "Mad World." Track 17 on *Donnie Darko Soundtrack* from the movie. Enjoy Records/Everloving Records. Released in 1982.

Springfield, Buffalo, singer, and Stephen Stills, songwriter. "For What It's Worth." Track 1 on *Buffalo Springfield*. ATCO records. Released in 1967.

Groban, Josh, singer, and Linda Thompson, songwriter. "You're Still You." Track 3 on *Josh Groban*. Reprise Records. Released in 2001.

Dylan, Bob. "Positively 4th Street" Track 9 on *Bob Dylan's Greatest Hits*. Originally released as a single 45. Columbia Records. Released in 1965.

REM, singer, M. Stipe, P. Buck, W. Berry, and M. Mills, songwriters. "Everybody Hurts" Track 4 on *Automatic for the People*. Warner Brothers. Released in 1982.

Guess Who, singer, and R. Bachman, songwriter. "Undun." Track 4 on *Canned Wheat*. RCA Victor Records. Released in 1969.

Barkley, Gnarls, singer, B. Burton, G. Reverberi, and T. Callaway, songwriters. "Crazy." Track 2 on *St. Elsewhere*. Downtown Records. Released in 2006.

Hornsby, Bruce. "The Way It Is." Track 5 on *The Way It Is*. RCA Records. Released in 1986.

Caillat, Colbie, singer-songwriter, B. James, J. B. Reeves, and K. B. Edmonds, songwriters. "Never Gonna Let You Down." Track 5 on *Gypsy Heart*. Sony/ATV Music, Warner Chappell Music. Released in 2014.

Simply Red, singer, Mick Hucknall, and N Moss, songwriters. "Holding Back the Years." Track 7 on *Picture Book*. WEA/Elektra Records. Released in 1985.

Genesis, singer, and Phil Collins, songwriter. "Misunderstanding." Track 5 on *Duke*. Atlantic Records. Released in 1980.

Menzel, Idina, singer, K Anderson-Lopez, R Lopez, songwriters. "Let It Go." Track 5 on *Frozen Soundtrack*. Walt Disney Records. Released in 2013.

Mike and the Mechanics, singer, Mike Rutherford, and C. Neil, songwriters. "All I Need Is a Miracle." Track 2 on *Mike and the Mechanics*. Atlantic Records. Released in 1985.

Henley, Don, singer-songwriter, M. Campbell, and J. D. Souther, songwriters. "Heart of the Matter." Track 10 on *End of the Innocence*. Geffen Records. Released in 1989.

Weekes, Des'ree, singer-songwriter, and A. Ingram, songwriter. "You Gotta Be" Track 3 on *I Ain't Moving*. Sony Soho Square Records. Released in 1994.

The Beatles, singer, J. Lennon, and P. McCartney, songwriters. "With a Little Help from My Friends." Track 2 on *Sgt. Pepper's Lonely Hearts Band*. Capitol Records. Released in 1967.

Chicago, singer, and J. Pankow, songwriter. "Just You N Me." Track 2 on *Chicago VI*. Columbia Records. Released in 1973.

Stewart, Rod, singer-songwriter, B. Dylan, J. Cregan, and K. Savigar, songwriters. "Forever Young." Track 4 on *Out of Order*. Warner Brothers Records. Released in 1988.

Hayes, Hunter, singer-songwriter, B. Baker, and K. Elam, songwriters. "Invisible." Track 5 on *Storyline*. Atlantic Records. Released in 2004.

Carlile, Brandi, singer-songwriter, D. Cobb, T. Hanseroth, and P. Hanseroth. "The Joke." Track 2 on *By the Way, I Forgive You*. Low Country/Elektra Records. Released in 2017.

DeShannon, Jackie, singer, B. Bacharach, and H. David, songwriters. "What the World Needs Now." Track 1 on *This Is Jackie DeShannon*. Imperial Records. Released in 1965.

The Beatles, singer, J. Lennon, and P. McCartney, songwriters. "Blackbird." Track 11 (3 on side two) on *White Album*. Apple Records. Released in 1968.

Edwards, Cliff, singer, L. Harline, and N. Washington, songwriters. "When You Wish upon a Star." Track 1 on Pinocchio Soundtrack. Walt Disney Music. Released in 1940.

Styx, singer, and D. DeYoung, songwriter. "Show Me the Way." Track 2 on *Edge of the Century*. A&M Records. Released in 1990.

Withers, Bill. "Lean on Me." Track 5 on *Still Bill*. Sussex Records. Released in 1972.

Petty, Tom, singer-songwriter, and Jeff Lynne, songwriter. "I Won't Back Down." Track 2 on *Full Moon Fever*. MCA Records. Released in 1988.

DeShannon, Jackie, singer-songwriter, J. Holiday, and R. Myers, songwriters. "Put a Little Love in Your Heart." Track 1 on *Put Little Love in Your Heart*. Imperial Records. Released in 1969.

Taylor, James, singer, and Carole King, songwriter. "You've Got a Friend." Track 2 on *Mud Slide Slim and the Blue Horizon*. Warner Brothers Records. Released in 1971.

The Beau Brummels, singer, and R. Elliott, songwriter. "Laugh Laugh." Track 1 on *Introducing the Beau Brummels*. Autumn Records. Released in 1965.

Elton, John, singer-songwriter, and B. Taupin. "I'm Still Standing." Track 2 on *Too Low for Zero*. Geffen Records. Released in 1993.

Streisand, Barbra, singer, L. Bernstein, and S. Sondheim, songwriter. "Somewhere (There's a Place)." Track 12 on *The Broadway Album*. Columbia Records. Released in 1985.

about the author

NONIE BOYES LIVES in a small town in Northwest Illinois. Nonie and her husband with forty-five years of marriage retired over a year and a half ago from a busy community to a farm-like atmosphere— big change but loving it!

Nonie was a preschool teacher for twenty-nine-plus years. She loved the children, classroom, and many teachers and families along the way. Always loved to write, many poems and children activity books (unpublished) were created over the years. Two wonderful children, their great spouses, and a handful of beautiful grandchildren equals a life filled with hope and gratitude.

CPSIA information can be obtained
at www.ICGtesting.com
Printed in the USA
BVHW080138240221
600893BV00008B/615